THE PLAYBOOK OF PRINCIPLES *for* Principals

RONNIE HARVEY JR.
PRINCIPAL "COACH" HARVEY

THE PLAYBOOK OF PRINCIPLES *for* Principals

RONNIE HARVEY JR.
PRINCIPAL "COACH" HARVEY

ISBN # 978-1-68593-122-3

Additional copies of this book are available from the Author

Ronnie Harvey | www.principalcoachharvey.com
Also Available on Amazon

CUSTOM BOOK MANUFACTURING SINCE 1982
809 East Napoleon St., Sulphur, Louisiana 70663 | 337-527-8308
books@wisepublications.biz
Visit our online Bookstore! **www.wisepublications.biz**

A game plan of best practices to empower, support, and guide principals working to shift the climate and culture of their school.

PRINCIPAL "COACH" HARVEY

PREFACE

Reading a book is like engaging in a conversation with the author. The approach to reading varies from one person to another. Some look for inspiration or motivation, while others approach it like a conference or seminar to gain knowledge. Many even discover a mentor or "COACH" within the pages, someone they can rely on for daily, weekly, or monthly guidance.

As I penned this book, I aimed to impart my coaching experience to a broad audience, employing the same voice I utilized with my students, faculty, staff, stakeholders, and school community. "The Playbook of Principles for Principals" is my brainchild, born out of a combination of strong passion and determination to impart value to those striving for progress and triumph. This book embodies my mission to elevate the lives of others, particularly in the sphere of education. I derive immense gratification from sharing my knowledge with fellow educators and empowering them to fortify their skills and enrich their experiences.

As an accomplished educator, I take immense pride in knowing my book will be an invaluable resource for educators worldwide. However, I cannot help but feel a tinge of hindrance with the limitations of traditional publishing. Once a book is printed, it remains static and unchanging, unable to keep up with the ever-evolving landscape of education and school leadership. If we were to discuss these topics personally, we would uncover new insights each time. I always strive to learn and grow, analyzing my mistakes to plan for the future. With each use of my book and "The Playbook of Principles for Principals Workbook," I am confident that you will discover something new and valuable to enhance your understanding of these critical current principles of today's leadership culture.

I regularly speak at conferences and events where I share the principles discussed in this book. I update my material frequently and love incorporating new stories and refining ideas. Presenting to different audiences also gives me fresh insights that further solidify my expertise. Drawing from my experiences as a teacher, coach, assistant principal, and principal, I am confident in my evolution. This book will be an invaluable resource for anyone looking to become a better principal, guiding them every step of the way.

Over time, the responsibilities of a principal have significantly evolved due to various academic accountability models at the federal, state, and district levels. These mandates ensure that schools meet or exceed local, state, and national education standards. As a result, the primary role of a principal, also known as "THE COACH," has shifted from building management and public relations to instructional leadership. Principals are now responsible for ensuring that all academic performance expectations are met while promoting a safe learning environment that supports students' physical, mental, social, and emotional well-being. Additionally, principals must prioritize systemic instructional coherence, meaning that every aspect of daily operations is aligned with improving student academic achievement.

As the principal, I made it my top priority to focus on instructional leadership. I carefully examined every aspect of the adults, actions, strategies, and factors involved to ensure academic success for our students. Our approach was based on a data-driven strategy addressing all student achievement aspects, such as test scores and accountability measures. With solid instructional leadership, we could improve school and student performance and confidently achieve our goals.

If you're a principal, consider The Playbook of Principles for Principals a vital tool. It is essential to implement intentional strategies to ensure the success and well-being of all students, parents, faculty, staff, and stakeholders. This playbook will help you position everyone to navigate and excel in today's constantly evolving environment of education and societal reforms. As a result, equipping yourself with this playbook is crucial to your success as a principal.

Becoming a successful principal requires adopting the "servant leader" mindset. This involves prioritizing the success of others and actively working to help them achieve it, leading to growth and progress. Effective leadership consists of a willingness to serve others. As a principal, your role is more than just a title; it's about using your influence to help others achieve their goals. Trust-building, commitment to people and processes, and selfless service are all qualities of a great principal. It is highly recommended that principals have a "bag," whether physical or mental. This bag allows them to carry all their necessary belongings securely. As a principal, it is crucial to first "secure the bag" and then bring it daily to ensure that all available resources can be utilized to advance EVERY CHILD in EVERY COMMUNITY and EVERY SCHOOL EVERY DAY. Securing the top bag ensures we are adequately equipped with the necessary resources.

As school leaders, our top priority is to protect our students, faculty, staff, stakeholders, and school community. Our bags must be top-quality, just like the best available bags on the market. They should be waterproof, lightweight, and flexible, ensuring that the tools inside can withstand all the ups and downs of being a school leader. By securing our principal bag and keeping our leadership toolkit close at hand, we can stay focused and ensure that we never forget "OUR WAY."

THE PURPOSE

The pathway of preparing, becoming, and leading as a principal is a unique experience. The daily journey to navigate principalship's dynamic subtleties and complexities can be overwhelming. As a principal, you are charged with recruiting, hiring, and retaining a highly effective educator workforce, leading shifts in the climate and culture of your school, counseling, evaluating, teaching, learning, and disciplining. Many of these feats can be exhausting and make you feel similar to having played an entire football game. This is why I developed *The Playbook of Principles for Principals.*

"THE PLAYBOOK OF PRINCIPLES FOR PRINCIPALS"

The Playbook confidently serves as an indispensable guide and valuable resource for those seeking to successfully implement school leadership at both the school and district levels. Additionally, it plays a vital role in fostering collaborative learning communities that share common values and principles. This playbook outlines several principles to follow. For each principle, I include the research behind it, summarize the key ideas, provide examples of how these principles are applied in schools, and offer real-life examples to illustrate these practices.

The Playbook of Principles for Principals will help you set yourself up for success for your rein as an aspiring administrator, assistant principal, or principal. Utilizing this impactful resource and employing strategies within the content will provide immediate benefits, resources, and tools to move your school forward, onward, and upward.

FORWORD

by Baruti K. Kafele

I have always consider the principalship to be a noble position. I would dare say that it is one of the most important positions on the planet. In all genres of organizations, leadership matters. Leadership is everything and that's inclusive of education from the superintendent to the principal. There's something about that principalship though. The principal is in the building with the teachers and students. The principal provides leadership for all aspects of the school. Looked at differently, everything and I mean everything that occurs in a school happens under the leadership of the principal. Translation – the buck stops with the principal. The principal is accountable for everything that happens under the roof of the school. That is a huge responsibility and it quite frankly requires a special individual who can simultaneously endure the pressures and demands that accompany school leadership while ensuring that teaching and learning are occurring at optimal levels. Continual professional learning, growth and development for the principal therefore matters exponentially.

The Playbook of Principles for Principals is the latest resource for providing the continual professional learning, growth and development that ongoing effective principal leadership requires. What I particularly admire about this book is that it is written by someone who has done the work…someone who has done the work at a very high level and under some extreme challenges. Principal Ronnie Harvey doesn't just "talk the talk" but he "lives the talk." He knows principal leadership first hand and as a result of his leadership effectiveness, he was selected Louisiana Secondary Schools Principal of the Year for 2022.

There's a ton of great information out there for school leadership development, but when the author is, or once was a practitioner….one who walked the walk…one who endured the challenges, obstacles, pressures and demands of school leadership…one who effectively elevated achievement or led the turnaround of a school, that's the book that I want to read. That's the book that Principal "Coach" Harvey has written for all of us. Principal Harvey has blessed us all with *The Playbook of Principles for Principals.*

CONTENTS

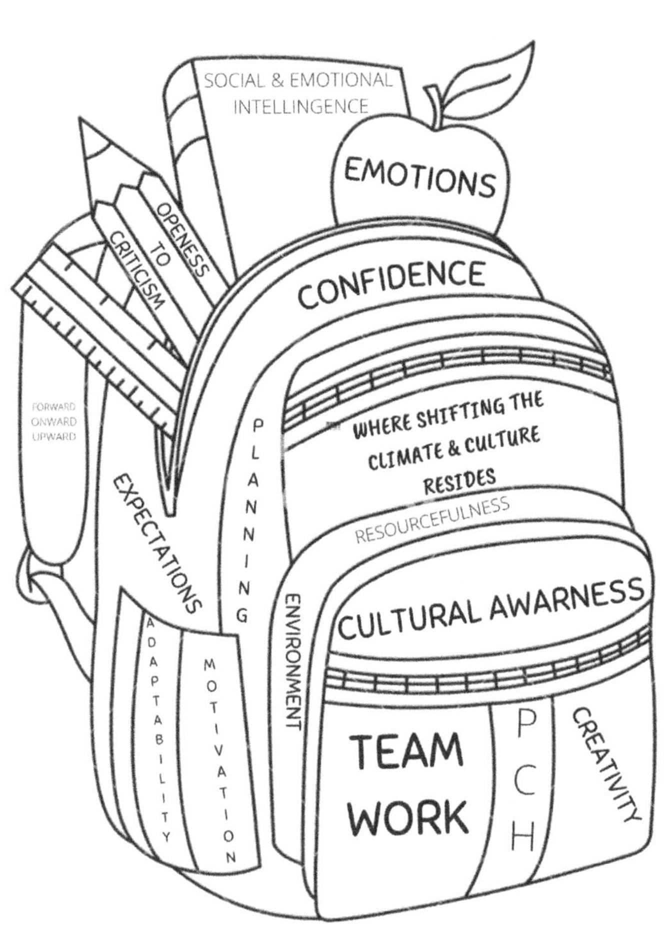

SOCIAL & EMOTIONAL INTELLIGENCE
EMOTIONS
OPENESS TO CRITICISM
CONFIDENCE
FORWARD
ONWARD
UPWARD
PLANNING
WHERE SHIFTING THE CLIMATE & CULTURE RESIDES
RESOURCEFULNESS
EXPECTATIONS
ENVIRONMENT
CULTURAL AWARNESS
ADAPTABILITY
MOTIVATION
TEAM WORK
PCH
CREATIVITY

The role of a principal has changed immensely over the years with the implementation of multiple federal, state, and district academic accountability models. Mandates have been in place to endure that schools are doing the job of educating children at a level that meets or exceeds local, state, and national standards. The primary role of the principal aka "THE COACH" has shifted from being primarily focused on building management and public relations to being the instructional leader of the building to ensuring all academic performance expectations are met. Principals must also ensure a laser-like focus on systemic instructional coherence so that every occasion, item, sequence, message, and minute of each day is aligned with improving student academic achievement in a physically, mentally, socially, and emotionally safe learning environment.

As a principal, instructional leadership was always a priority of my daily regime. Instructional leadership examines the evidence and impact each adult, action, strategy, and factor has on student academic achievement. To get the outcome you desire, you must use data-driven strategies and actions to make an impact on each factor in regard to student achievement in terms of test scores and standardized accountability measures. Instructional leadership not only matters but is a priority in school leadership and school/student performance.

The Playbook of Principles for Principals is a must-have for your "Principal Bag" Your bag as a principal should contain resources/tools that lead to intentional strategies to strategically and thoughtfully elevate all students, parents, faculty, staff, and stakeholders. Position everyone with a vested interest in children to ensure that they not only survive but thrive within the ever-changing landscape of society and education reforms.

Being a principal and experiencing success doesn't occur if the desire to be a "servant leader" is not part of your fabric. Servant leadership is about service to others, it is a choice, a decision to put others ahead of yourself to help them be successful, ultimately moving them forward, onward, and upward. Being a principal is more than a title of position; it's about influence and the willingness to help others achieve their goals.

Great principals build trust, are committed to people and processes, and are dedicated to selfless service. This is why every principal should have "A BAG," whether it's a physical one or a mental one. Most people carry a bag because it allows them to their belongings safely. As a principal, we must first "SECURE THE BAG," then carry it daily so that we can be ready to utilize all resources that it contains to move EVERY CHILD forward, onward, and upward in EVERY COMMUNITY, EVERY SCHOOL, EVERY DAY! Securing the principal bag ensures that we are adequately given and equipped with resources that allows us to protect the most prize possession we are responsible for; our students, faculty and staff, stakeholders, and school community. Just like the best available bags on the market, our bags must be waterproof, lightweight, and flexible, and they provide maximum. In other words, we must be sure that the tools inside our bag can withstand the good times and bad times that come with being a school leader. Securing the principal bag is utilizing it means that you are being intentional and ensuring that the leadership toolkit is kept close and ready to assist, making it difficult to lose focus or forget "YOUR WAY."

PRE-GAME OVERVIEW

SAY IT LOUD AND CLEAR

PRE-GAME OVERVIEW

Say it loud and clear

COMMUNICATE

The expectation to set the tone, and create the atmosphere.
What time is it? GAMETIME!

Many times, the loudest person in the room can often be depicted as the most crucial person, and for many reasons. However, if the person has a meaningful message, they can dictate the group of people who are listening in a positive and empowering way. So, it's time for all players (Faculty, staff, students, stakeholders, district leaders, and all academic components that impact your school) to enter the locker room for the big game. Fasten your tie, grab your coat, and straighten your lapel pin. Then, it's time for you to execute your plan of action to make the school you lead a better place to teach, learn, and work.

Every principal should have a guidebook, in other words, a playbook that can be used to guide them through the day, week, month, and entire school year. The Playbook of Principles for Principals is a tool that you can utilize to lead and win the day every day! Educators and school leaders need support and guidance to build successful schools and ensure they meet the needs of ALL students. The Playbook of Principles of Principals is specifically designed to support principals, assistant principals, and aspiring principals. The playbook is dedicated to helping train, grow, and coach the next generation of educational and instructional leadership.

While being a principal can be stressful and often underappreciated, it can also be one of the most rewarding experiences anyone will encounter. You can positively impact children every day and for generations to come.

Be the role model every child deserves, the person that sees more in them than they ever imagined, and the person who will never give up on them. Every principal should develop a personal mission statement that aligns with the school's mission statement. A mission statement is what drives the principal/school. It is what you do daily throughout the business, and from it comes the objectives and, finally, what it takes to reach them. It also shapes the school's identity and establishes the framework. The effects of a good mission statement confirm its value at any school and must be communicated early and often. By its definition, you can quickly see how a solid mission statement can motivate any team to advance toward the goal because they started at the same place and are working together to reach the same purpose.

Now that you have effectively established the mission for yourself as a principal and your school, in continuing to affect communication, you must make everyone aware of the vision for yourself and your school. Your vision statement gives everyone a sense of direction. It is the future of the professional in you and the outlook for the school that provides the sole purpose. The vision statement is about what you would like to become. It›s aspirational and should be motivational!

The vision statement promotes growth, both externally and internally. A strong vision statement helps teams focus on what matters for their school and, most importantly, their school. It also invites innovation. Purpose-driven principals envision success because they know what success means for their school and all stakeholders.

You are probably wondering; they both sound the same! Is there a difference?

Absolutely! The vision statement focuses on the next day or tomorrow and what the school wants to become. The mission statement focuses on the moment right now or today and what the school does in real-time. While schools commonly use mission and vision statements interchangeably, having both is important. One only works with the other because having purpose and meaning is critical. When addressing your team in the pre-game speech, be sure that you are very strategic when voicing your commitments. Decisions that have long-term impacts take time to reverse. These decisions differ from tactical decisions, which have a short-term effect and are easier to change. Strategic commitments influence the nature of competition in education, and competitive dynamics regarding assessments and daily logistics evolve.

For principals to be effective daily, a commitment must be made to be visible, understandable, and credible.

In a school, Strategic Commitments guide the organization›s process and cycle of continuous improvement. They can be a reference for making all decisions, just as this playbook is for a principal. Your mission statement, vision statement, core values, and strategic commitments should focus on anything you set out to do as a principal. Effective communication is a crucial dimension of leadership as a principal. Effective communication reinforces the knowledge, skills, and personalities of principals who are required to have a direct and indirect influence on student outcomes and student outcomes while setting the tone daily. Develop a system of processes FAST! Make it a key priority to develop a plan of strategies for how you will handle the communication that comes in and out of the school office. Spend time early on with your office staff (administrative assistant, clinic, counselor, food service, custodial, athletic,s), and be sure you have identified communication processes for all areas of the school: parent communication, weekly communication to staff, delays, inside vs. outside recess (elementary), cleaning protocols, etc. Inventory this team often to be sure you have functioning systems to alleviate headaches early into your principalship.

Overall, the best way to control the atmosphere and communicate effectively is to utilize some of the following:

FACE-TO-FACE COMMUNICATION

- Always listen carefully and make every attempt not to interrupt. Always think about how much you would like or dislike this conversation.
- Be grateful and constantly show appreciation for your critics.
- Treat each conversation as crucial to ensure your agendas are applied, and take full advantage of face-to-face meetings to initiate new discussions about things of importance to you, your vision, and your school.
- Always take notes and have a third-party if possible. The document agreed on times and dates. Put follow-up actions in your calendar.
- Work to try and reduce your use of conversation fillers like 'um' and 'er,' as well as common phrases such as 'you know, 'basically,' 'to be honest, at the end of the day, 'the fact of the matter is.
- Difficult conversations with adults will occur. Don't become defensive – breathe and count to 10.

PERSONAL

- Your mood, actions, and demeanor
- Your body language, moods, and actions convey potent communication.
- It is a must that you have confidence in what you are saying and doing. Studies suggest that others are more likely to agree with your proposal if you appear confident. Conversely, the less secure you appear in your message, the more objections you will likely meet.

- A leader failing to complete a routine task suggests the routine is not essential. Similarly, failure to follow through on a goal or promise will undermine your credibility. Ensure the link between what you say and what you do remains close. If a disparity develops between them for any reason, explain why.
- Remaining approachable while being regarded and consulted as a professional leader with significant knowledge about teaching and learning requires principals to maintain a cheerful demeanor even if the going is tough. The irritability of a principal can quickly permeate their campus.
- As a school leader, you must never forget that you are now a public figure and will be subject to much more criticism than you were as a teacher or regular educator. Therefore, always strive to be consistent, clear, and transparent so that all community members know that what they see is what they get. Take pride in answering questions, discussing the school vision and goals, and listening attentively to all community members.

PHONE CALLS AND EMAILS

- Treat calls and emails as an essential part of the job. These are often the first experience people have of your school.
- Have an enthusiastic phone voice and manner, even on the worst day.
- Identify yourself.
- Use the email subject line to your advantage, that is, as a summary.
- Put aside time to answer phone calls and emails. Putting the email subject line helps you with time management. Publicize the best time to ring in newsletters.

- Answer phone messages and emails within 24 hours but take your time with answers you need to consider.
- Try for a balance of five calls home to praise students for every one critical.
- Ensure that the school's answer phone messages, music, and so on are aligned with its goals and context. Make them warm, welcoming, and inclusive.

COMMUNICATION CHANNELS

Internet Presence

- Where does your school stand in terms of its digital footprint? You and the school-level administrators have ultimate responsibility for it.
- Decide whether you need to be an open or closed channel and for whom.
- You should choose platforms that are easy to use for both your school and the audience(s).
- You should present your content concisely, professionally, and safely. For instance, you should not post images of children without their parent's permission.
- Verify that the content reinforces your school's key messages, values, and beliefs.
- Manage the content according to protocols.
- More than one person must create content, moderate it, and monitor inappropriate responses.

School Events

- Every event is an excellent opportunity for communication.
- Consider cultural reflection and responsibility when planning events.
- Meeting and greeting as many parents and community members as possible are essential.
- Only talk for a short time. Keep sight of your school's current goals and student achievement. Clarify what the school's core business is.
- Reward students for their effort and achievement by including them and making them feel had.
- Acknowledge and thank parents and stakeholders for supporting students' learning.

Newsletters

- Newsletters may be digital or paper. Find out how parents, community members, and stakeholders wish to be informed about school events. Provide a variety of options.
- School newsletters must inform, promote, gather, and educate the community. Identify how you want each newsletter's balance to work.
- Your news should be brief, to the point, and customized. Today, people are dealing with a great deal of information. But, increasingly, people are discerning when it comes to consuming information.
- Communicate your school's vision, values, strategies, and plans through the newsletter.

Align the messages to support your crucial leadership activities: leading change, leading learning, and problem-solving.

- Establish a regular publication schedule and stick to it.
- Preparing each edition is easier if you use a template.
- Recruit others to collect copies, for example, students and staff.
- It's essential to have quality but keep your budget in mind. Maintain the highest level of accuracy in detail and grammar. Have a neutral proofreader.
- Ensure the school has parental permission to use any photos of students.
- Schedule a specific time for your part of the newsletter, preferably several days before publication.
- Ensure digital newsletters are easy to read online or download and open.
- Your newsletters fall under your overall responsibility. Therefore, it would be best if you had the final say on what will be included and how it is said.

Now that it is almost time to begin the game, you have discovered how to use your voice and be clear about it. Commit to making it all make sense to both you and your team. Communication is a two-way street. However, just as you say it loud and clear, you must listen close.

Listening

Effective communication is a two-way process. It is important to remember that you will learn more by listening than by speaking and that people will only open up to you if you are good at listening.

Consider: focusing on the moment and the person speaking – adopting a listening attitude.

- Avoid distractions, for example, moving away from your computer and putting away your phone.
- Always start by asking questions instead of trying to provide answers. It will show that you are giving full attention to what the other individual is saying and not just entertaining the moment.
- Focus on seeking clarification and explanation, especially if the speaker's tone is somewhat critical, instead of focusing on what you want to hear.
- Getting clarity and agreement by reiterating what they said sends an indication of whose voices have been omitted or underrepresented.
- Embrace a listening approach to the noise of learning at your school, such as an indication of analysis, interest, earnest endeavor, shared thinking and teamwork, and teacher help sounds of other teachers' approach to teaching, such as team teaching, participation in PLC's, collaborative planning, and support.
- Find a logical person or ear for the noise you want to hear that is present when you need to attend but would prefer to avoid hearing at the current time or place. Please keep all the sounds and information in your memory about the school and use them at appropriate times to make progress on developments as much!

(Coaching Point) THE TRANSITION

To make your transition into your new situation as seamless as possible, position:

1. Familiarize yourself with the school before your first day.
2. Consider inviting the outgoing principal for lunch or visiting the school while students are present.
3. Take the time to listen and observe, noting what is thriving and may need improvement.
4. Walk the building with your predecessor to provide a sense of continuity for teachers and students.

It's crucial to remember the names of the teachers you meet, and if necessary, a cheat sheet can be created. Remember to express gratitude towards parents and teachers involved in the interview process. Maintaining a frequent smile is essential, as it can be daunting to have a new boss. A seamless transition will help alleviate any worries.

During the summer, meeting with parents and teachers individually or in small groups is a great opportunity. This can help build valuable relationships that are often challenging to establish during the busy school year. When meeting new colleagues, listening attentively and speaking thoughtfully is essential. Be open about your educational aspirations and values, but remember to use discretion. What you say may be shared with others through their perspectives.

Leaving your current school on a positive note can help you transition smoothly to your new one. Consider organizing a farewell party and going with good vibes. Remember that the education industry is small, so the connections you make at your old school may be helpful in your future professional life.

YOUR THOUGHTS:

1ST QUARTER

WITH THE PLAN IN HAND, **EXECUTE** WHAT YOU HAVE BEEN PRACTICING FOR.

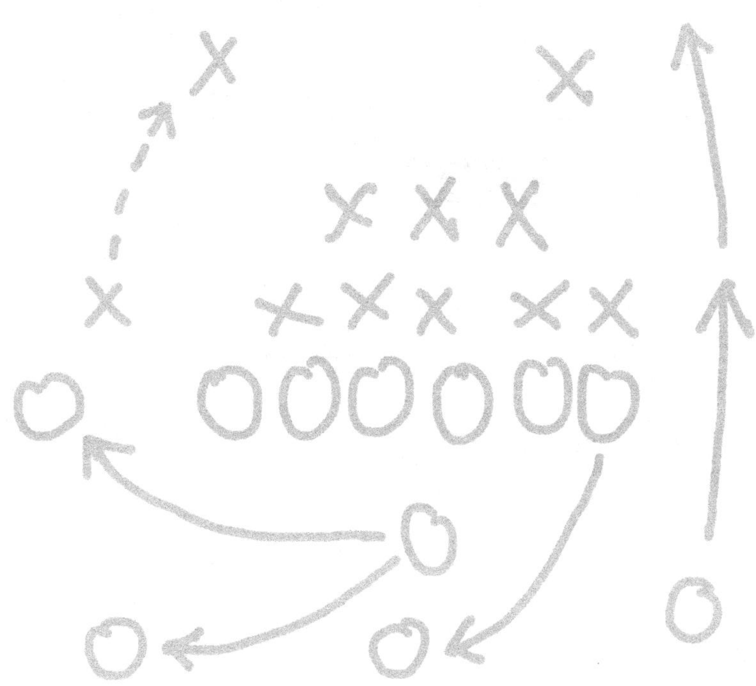

1ST QUARTER

With the plan in hand, EXECUTE what you have been practicing for.

The moment we all have been waiting for is finally here! School leader, you're on the clock! I remember my first principalship thinking this is going to be a breeze! Stay late, work hard, get great results, and shine! Boy, was I wrong? To be a great principal, you must first know how to be a PRINCIPAL. Keep who you are. Here is the best advice I wish someone had given me when I was in your shoes. Keep who you are as a person. Avoid allowing your school principal to overshadow your identity. It's easy to do. You are out in the community—at events, on various not-for-profit boards, or even at the grocery store—and people will recognize you quickly as "that's The Principal." But be sure to keep in your life what brings your personal to let your school become your work and your hobby, although I am very guilty of making this colossal mistake then and even more so now. Keep the balance between school and life to ensure optimal success in all areas of life.

As a principal, you must remember that time is always of the essence. Lost seconds lead to days of being behind and missing deadlines.

KEEP THE PAPER MOVING.

- Don't let a piece of paper sit on your desk for too long. Please put it in a file to be dealt with later, pass it along, or throw it away. Keep things simple by only handling them once.

- Utilize your administration support so you are one of many who know where things are.

DECLUTTER YOUR WORK AREA.

- You'll feel more in control of your life once you do it.

BE HIGHLY PRODUCTIVE IN SHORT BURSTS.

- This gets paperwork done.
- Know your best times for getting things done – use them, and ensure others know this is how you work.

USE YOUR LAPTOP TO SAVE TIME.

- Establish a simple system for storing and retrieving data, ideas, plans, budgets, and letters.

CONTROL INTERRUPTIONS.

- Responses to voicemail and email should be limited to once or twice daily.
- Identify and maintain periods when the door is closed, such as early mornings and after 5:00 pm. Use these as high-productivity sessions.

Proper preparation will always ensure good performance.

RATHER THAN PLANNING YOUR APPOINTMENTS AND WEEKLY SCHEDULE DAILY, PREPARE THEM A MONTH IN ADVANCE.

- Be prepared for the unexpected.
- Establish routines for regular activities, such as board reports, by keeping an eye on the calendar.

TAKE A LONG-TERM VIEW.

- Working on a strategic task over months, such as a building project, is sometimes necessary. Such studies need close attention, so plan time for them.

PRIORITIZE LONG-TERM AND SHORT-TERM GOALS.

- Make sure they are easily accessible by keeping them in a convenient location.
- It is essential to consider these factors to use your time best.

ANTICIPATE AND KEEP AHEAD.

- Consider how you might handle annual routines in the future based on how you take them now.

AVOID PROCRASTINATION.

- When large jobs are broken down into smaller ones, they are easier to handle.
- You will only waste more time if you put off a big task now.

ORGANIZE YOUR TASKS BY WRITING THEM DOWN.

- Most principals swear by these.
- Writing down tasks and prioritizing them will help you focus your time.
- Reprioritize as circumstances change – do this with your long- and short-term priorities in mind.
- To-do lists should not be kept in your email inbox.

SET AGENDAS FOR MEETINGS.

- Organize your meetings in advance to achieve your goals. Discussions that are poorly planned waste time and resources

DELEGATE. DELEGATE. DELEGATE.

Always remember that you can delegate duties, but you can never delegate responsibility. Always remember you're the principal and cannot trust that title!

MAKE A DELEGATION.

- There is no need to do everything yourself. You can delegate many system processes, including finance, property, and staff management.
- If you need help leading a meeting or writing a policy, ask someone else. In addition, this helps others develop their leadership abilities.

Ensure you delegate effectively to your teachers and management team members if you have them. Sometimes, they are better at what they do than you are. Delegation does not mean abdication; it just implies confidence in their abilities.

Put your trust in your employees.

- Build your staff's confidence and independence to control the team's flow through your door.
- Be supportive of genuine responsibility and delegated tasks, even if they aren't precisely done as you would.
- Try to reduce any over-dependence on your decision-making.
- Make sure your administrative staff is empowered to make decisions by giving them even a tiny amount of time.
- Be respectful and considerate of these close supporters if you want the school to succeed.

Engage your staff in a team-based approach.

- By setting this expectation, work can be shared more efficiently, and rework will be less likely.
- Make sure daily decisions and actions are based on the school's goals and plans regarding teaching and learning.

Seek assistance.

- Consider hiring additional support staff or rearranging their responsibilities and time to free up your time for team development, teaching, and building relationships.

Time management for others

It would be best to remember that everyone's emergency isn't always yours, no matter how bad it sounds. Particular attention should be paid to managing time pressures created by others. Unexpected events often require changing priorities and adjusting priorities. You may receive phone calls, visitors who need to be scheduled, mail that you didn't request, or even meetings you didn't ask for. It can also be a problem for staff and administrative team members to pass the buck. Keeping things in perspective is your responsibility, so don't rush.

It is important to remind others that education is not an emergency industry regularly. Make sure you do not make quick decisions because of someone else's schedule. Instead, say, "I'll get back to you in an hour or whatever, but specify a time."

A media organization or other organization that wants your response is particularly likely to do this. They can wait. Thinking things through is the best course of action.

Sometimes, you have to close the open door.

- It is not necessary for parents and visitors to see you all the time. To inform the wider school community about whom to contact, use newsletters or an email tree managed by another staff member. For example, a secretary may be able to direct visitors to another part of the school in larger schools.
- Small school principals often spend most of their release time attending scheduled and unscheduled appointments. Inform your community that you are not always available except in an emergency.

Keep an open mind and listen carefully.

- Practice active and critical listening frequently, saving you time.
- Be clear about your available time: "I have set aside 20 minutes [for example] - is that okay with you?"
- If you specify a duration, they will be more likely to be concise, and it will be easier for you to focus on what they say.

Make sure that responsibilities are placed where they should be.

- Keep the delegation principles above when helping staff and the administrative team solve their problems.
- Consistent learning and professional development must be your best friend and the guiding tool for success.

Invest time and effort in your learning.

- You need to make time for learning as an educational leader.
- Over the coming year, identify areas of skill or knowledge you wish to improve or develop. Make these priorities part of your appraisal process.

Remove yourself.

- Successful reflection requires time and space. Leaving the school altogether enables better review. Taking 10 minutes from your desk can clear your head and give you time to think. See what's happening around the school by taking a walk around it.
- Reflection time, mentoring, and professional learning groups are time-saving activities that increase your team's capacity and reduce time pressures on you in the long term.

Please refresh your mind.

- Your brain can learn and solve problems better by regularly allocating time for mental and physical refreshments.
- Investment in refreshments helps increase productivity.
- Access easy links to learning sources.

Make your learning time more efficient by recording or saving valuable resources. Learning from other people online or through written sources is possible. Ensure you can access these sources with a few mouse clicks or by calling them.

As we continue preparing to execute this game plan, we must remember that it doesn't matter the type of players on our team. Whether good or bad, rookie or veteran, team player or team destroyer, the only thing that matters is the RESULTS. Excuses never lead to better solutions. Instead, utility excuses create a barrier preventing execution and distract us from getting the desired results as leaders.

One of the first excuses for failure is far too often blame the kids. We don't control which students walk through our doors each day; it's our job to educate them to the best of our ability. While some people in the school may not believe it, every parent sends us the best kid they have. They don't have a better kid locked up at home that will make straight A's and never misbehaves. The one we get in our classrooms is the best they have to send. We need to control the proficiency or performance level they come to us on. The goal is to reach and teach them, to make at least a year's growth in a year, and even more if students come to us below grade level proficiency to help close the achievement gap. There's always the excuse for more resources, to which we must ask, "Is it truly a lack of resources or resourcefulness?" The truth is that the best leaders and teachers find a way to be successful. After blaming the students, the parents are often the next ones to be accused. "If we had more parental involvement? If our parents made the kids do their work? If they produced and raised smarter kids?" Parents generally do the best they know how to do, and we must help them be able to do more to support them.

This is often only a factor within our control if we go to great lengths or exhaust extensive resources. Wouldn't that vast amount of time and resources generate far more significant results if they were spent on students? But, unfortunately, you only have a limited amount of time and resources, and it's part of instructional coherence to ensure they are spent where they can yield the most positive impacts on student learning.

To combat this matter, I created an initiative called *"Parent Night School with Principal Coach Harvey."* This resource was created to engage parents the same we engage students by TEACHING THEM.

As a principal, you must develop the mindset of meeting parents where they are instead of expecting parents where they are not. Many parents want to be great, like teachers, assistant principals, and principals. However, we all know this task is challenging, and we can only sometimes create a blanket approach of one size fits all.

Principals too often place blame on the teachers. The truth is that most teachers are doing their best, and it's the job of the principal, and instructional leader, to ensure all teaching and learning is effective and help support/build capacity when needed. Great principals hire, train, motivate, and retain great teachers. There's the excuse of the curriculum and standards requiring more challenging and more items to complete from the central office staff or district personnel. It seems logical and makes sense for the instruction to be rigorous if it's supposed to prepare to graduate students to be globally competitive. There's an excuse to add more technology or the latest instructional ideas. Still, the data doesn't support this either as enhancing student learning significantly. So we've tried to fix the students, the parents, the teachers, the principals, the finances and resources, and the infrastructure? After all this blame about what needs to be fixed, we've yet to solve the problem and improve what we can control. The fact remains that assigning blame never fixes a problem. As a team, we are accountable for our results; we must spend our time and resources doing things that will significantly impact student learning. Find a way to be successful. We all have that capacity if we want it bad enough. The research is already out there that tells us what to do and how to do it; the doing is up to us, in any case! It's time to stop making excuses and find a way to get results. In the end, the results are what we will be judged by!

The fact remains that assigning blame never fixes a problem. As a team, we will all be held accountable for our results; we must spend our time and resources doing things that will significantly impact student learning. Find a way to be successful; we all have that capacity if we want it bad enough. The research is already out there that tells us what to do and how to do it. The doing is up to us, however! It's time to stop making excuses and find a way to get results. In the end, the results are what we will be judged by!

(Coaching Point) Build Relationships

Effective school leadership relies on solid relationships as its foundation. Building and nurturing these relationships is critical. Before the school year starts, try to get to know everyone in your community. Share personal information about your family and hobbies to show your human side. When meeting with teachers, visit them in their classrooms and staff rooms, where they feel comfortable. Try to connect with quieter teachers and show respect to those who may not be entirely supportive. Most importantly, listen attentively to your staff to demonstrate how much their opinions and input are valued.

Connecting with various school community members, such as custodians, bus drivers, lunchroom supervisors, non-certified staff, and parent leaders of organizations like PTA or booster clubs is essential. However, it's especially crucial to establish a positive and robust relationship with the school secretary, as they can be a valuable ally or a challenging obstacle depending on the rapport you build with them.

To succeed in your district, building relationships with other principals is essential. They can serve as mentors and guide you through the district's culture. Additionally, it's crucial to establish partnerships with district office personnel, as they can help you navigate through any mistakes you may make. Finally, having allies in the central office can also be invaluable when advocating for critical issues.

Each person you collaborate with has a unique personal story, family, and aspirations. Take the initiative to connect with them on those levels by sharing some of your dreams. Embrace vulnerability as it showcases your relatable human side rather than a sign of weakness.

YOUR THOUGHTS:

PRINCIPLE I.

Take what's available: EVALUATE your talent, and strategically make moves based on your personnel.

As a principal, you must be able to accept and win with the hand that you are dealt. Therefore, as a principal, one of my main "sayings', is that we use diversity to overcome adversity in recruiting, hiring, and retaining highly qualified/certified individuals.

Often, we hear school administrators state that they need better teachers, staff, students, parents, facilities, etc. However, the solutions we seek are often inside the people we already have on our staff. It's all about motivating your team. Encouraging teachers to power through tough times is essential to your school's success.

Among a principal›s many responsibilities is the critical task of encouraging and building up their teachers to face and overcome any obstacle they encounter. Research shows that a principal›s ability to lead and motivate their teachers impacts retention positively. If you want to keep good teachers, you must make them want to stay. The best way to make good teachers stay is to provide the support and motivation they need to do their job. Sure, telling your educators they have your full support is easy. However, when motivating teachers — and their students — organization is the key to success. Planners are a crucial tool for educators and students. You can organize lesson plans, assignments, deadlines, and events with a planner. When juggling everything simultaneously, you need a place to put all the information and refer to it whenever required. There are a million little ways to encourage your teachers, but if you want to know how to motivate teachers, it all comes down to 10 simple things.

PRAISE

Take the time to call attention to a teacher who has gone above and beyond. Sure, this can be done via email, but making a public gesture of thanks goes a long way toward making teachers feel good about themselves. Each time you have a staff meeting, mention a few teachers who've contributed, especially in the last month or two. Send an email of thanks after a group of teachers has organized an event or successful program. That being said, don't get so focused on praising the individual that you forget to thank others around them. Make a point to organize "thank you" breakfasts or lunches for departments or all the teachers to show thanks for their hard work.

ENCOURAGE TEACHERS TO MOTIVATE EACH OTHER

Even in a smaller school, you can only be everywhere at a time. Teachers see and hear things that you don't. So get them involved in developing activities to motivate and reward colleagues for a well-done job. For example, implement a "Teacher of the Month" system where teachers vote for one colleague who has gone above and beyond. Or, implement a pay-it-forward system where you celebrate one teacher for his efforts, then that teacher selects another teacher to honor the next month. Another great way to motivate educators is to pair older, more experienced teachers with new ones in a teacher-to-teacher mentorship program. The program can encourage more experienced educators to provide advice and support to people who are just entering the field. Organize the program and watch the pairings to ensure both teachers benefit from their connection.

BE AVAILABLE

Your primary role as a school administrator is to do whatever it takes to free up your teachers to teach. Talk to them. Find out what they're struggling with, what's falling through the cracks, and what they could help with. Ask what your teachers want in a principal. Then, with their permission, jump in and help. It could be something as simple as returning books to the school library after a class is through. Or, it could be something more time-consuming, such as working through a conflict with a parent. The key here is to ask your teachers how you can help them. If you start doing stuff, they may think you're micromanaging or watching them so that you can critique them later. Instead, set their minds at ease by communicating your desire to support their day-to-day activities. While you cannot change things like class size, limited funding, or student behavior, you can offer your teachers a listening ear. It may be counterproductive to have an open-door policy, so consider instituting office hours. Set specific hours each day or each week when your teachers know your door is open. They can stop by to talk about whatever is on their mind — a new idea, questions about lesson planning, requests for new equipment, or concerns about a student. When your teachers know you're available and listening to them, they'll be more likely to help when you ask or take on a new task when needed.

SOCIAL EVENTS OUTSIDE OF SCHOOL

When you know someone personally, it's easier to understand what makes them tick. You can better see how their strengths and weaknesses shape their abilities in the workplace. Make a point to organize — and attend — social events outside of school hours. Host a holiday party for the teachers at your home or a local restaurant. Organize an end-of-the-year barbecue at your neighborhood pool. When you take the time to get to know your teachers and even their families, you build a stronger relationship that will translate into more motivation in the workplace. Spending time together outside of school can also go a long way in understanding the individual personalities of each person on your staff. You learn a lot by meeting someone's child or spouse. You can know much about someone by learning something as simple as their upbringing. Even Christmas party small talk can go a long way toward providing your teacher's emotional support during the most challenging weeks at school.

PROFESSIONAL DEVELOPMENT OPPORTUNITIES

Even if your district requires teachers to meet specific professional development requirements, looking for ways to go beyond those is a good idea. For example, you can help teachers find relevant courses, workshops, or conferences to attend outside of school. Please try to get information and present it to teachers through emails or during staff meetings. Beyond providing the information, you can also approve their requests to attend these programs by offering financial assistance and agreeing to travel away from school when needed.

SUPPORT YOUR TEACHER IN FRONT OF PARENTS

Supporting your teachers in front of parents

As an administrator, a large part of your job is dealing with student conflicts. Often, this will involve parents. Sometimes, a child may struggle in a class, and the parent is worried. In other cases, a student may have started a fight in the hallway or stolen something from another student. Whatever the case, you and the teacher will likely have several conversations with that student's parents. Sometimes parents become very defensive about their children and may become angry and frustrated with you or the teacher. No matter what is said, when you talk with a student or parent, you should support your teacher's initial actions to correct the situation. Your job is to keep your teachers, and it starts by having their back when it's against the wall. If the teacher didn't handle the situation well, privately discuss what they could have done differently.

RESPECT THEIR TIME

One of the best ways a principal can motivate their teachers is by showing respect for their time — both during and after school. Refrain from scheduling staff meetings and professional development workshops in the week leading up to report cards or final exams. Don't pile on extra paperwork during standardized testing week. Recognize that there are just certain times of the school year that are stressful. Your teachers' last need is to feel you don't understand that. So, rather than adding more to their plate, stop and ask how you can make things easier. Make a coffee run during a teacher's workday or set up donuts in the teacher's lounge. Lend a hand grading papers or setting up testing when you can. Another important way to respect your teachers' time is to encourage organization. Even in this digital age, encourage your teachers to keep a detailed daily calendar to keep track of their time and responsibilities. There are many benefits to using a traditional paper planner, including a greater chance of remembering what they need to do!

GIVE THANK YOU GIFTS

While it's essential to tighten the school budget where possible, consider setting aside a small amount each year for teacher gifts. When a teacher goes above and beyond — giving up their planning period to cover a sick teacher's class or organizing a school-wide food drive — show your appreciation with a small gift, such as a $5 Starbucks card or a small bag of chocolates. The point is to show your team that their hard work hasn't gone unnoticed. If the school budget doesn't allow for tangible gifts, get creative. When a teacher goes above and beyond, hand them a coupon that offers to cover one class period within the semester. When they cash in on it, you agree to spend the period with their class. Although it's not a day off or a monetary reward, there's not a teacher out there who wouldn't relish an extra planning period or extended lunch once in a while. And the thought of earning an hour of free time may become a great motivator among your teachers!

INCLUDE TEACHERS IN STRATEGIC PLANNING

Teachers want their students to learn. So they are vested in school reforms and changes that help students understand better. When teachers are given a chance to offer input and guidance toward shaping school policy, they often feel more motivated in their teaching and participation.

This can be especially important if you're in a school looking to improve student achievement, but it rings true just about anywhere. It's also a good idea to keep teachers in the loop about what's going on at the district level, especially if many new policies are coming to a vote that will affect them later.

In some cases, they may have seen news coverage about controversial issues, which makes it even more important to include them in school-level discussions when possible. And in some cases, it's a good idea to encourage them to speak up and make their voices heard by the local school board. If an issue can't be addressed at the school level, there's nothing wrong with helping your teachers advocate for themselves and their students. A good principal can guide their advocacy reasonably and respectfully.

MENTORING

Although teachers can — and should — be encouraged to motivate each other, there's also a lot to be said for a principal mentoring their teachers. Mentoring provides significant motivation for teachers because it guides them toward a stronger and more successful teaching career. To do this, a principal must always be learning. A good principal stays abreast of the latest educational theories and practices and then shares them with their teachers, helpfully and practically to implement. In some cases, you may look for ways to mentor teachers one-on-one. However, it's probably more helpful to work with small groups, such as during teacher-staff meetings or in short exchanges with the various departments in your school. That said, you don't have to lead after-school seminars about educational theory or spend hours pouring over the latest publications. A good principal works smarter, not harder. Remember those newer teachers in your school? They've probably just come from university classrooms where they were introduced to educational theories your veteran teachers may not be as familiar with. Tap those newcomers to share their knowledge with their colleagues during a staff meeting. The point of a principal-teacher mentorship isn't to sit down face-to-face with every teacher every week. It's to find ways to help teachers find the knowledge and support they need to do their job well.

(Coaching Point) LEARN THE CULTURE

The culture of a school is like the atmosphere everyone experiences without realizing it. So when a new principal starts, they must become a student of the culture to understand how things are done in the school.

Before officially starting at a school, paying attention to small details that can reveal a lot about the school's culture is essential. During visits or meetings with teachers, observe the parking lot during dismissal to see if teachers leave before all buses have finished loading students or if they stay to help. Take note of how the school celebrates holidays and staff birthdays and whether students are allowed in the faculty lounge. These observations can provide valuable insights into the school's culture. The initiation process for new teachers or students joining the school follows specific organization, scheduling, and responsibilities guidelines. It's crucial to respect the school culture, even if it differs from your approach. Pep rallies, graduations, and in-service days in August are all included in this process.

If your school has a toxic culture, it's essential to make changes gradually. A toxic culture can harm teacher relationships, leading to gossip instead of communication and discipline, becoming a power struggle that negatively affects students and teachers. It's your responsibility to work towards restoring a healthy school environment.

Transforming the culture of a school is a challenging and time-consuming task. As a new principal, it is crucial to maintain your integrity and improve your listening skills to facilitate effective communication. Genuine concern for your colleagues and regular and transparent communication are critical components of a thriving culture. Being patient is essential as building a healthy school culture takes time, and you cannot expect to achieve it overnight.

YOUR THOUGHTS:

PRINCIPLE II

Be METHODICAL in your approach and decisions.

When making decisions, always remember that leaders must be intentional and methodical regarding decision-making. Leadership only succeeds if the leader brings other people with the same vision and can all work together and trust one another. A school in deep trouble will take years to change, and it must be a continuous process with continual support. And that means it can't be one person but a group dedicated enough to stay with something for an extended period. This chapter explores the decision-making strategies that school principals employ while dealing with the challenges faced during the change process at their schools. Decision-making is a significant management process and stands out as one of the most critical responsibilities of principals. It involves choosing the most reasonable view or alternative from various perspectives and options related to an issue and making a judgment to attain the desired results. There has been a significant shift in the landscape of the principalship over the past few decades, documenting evolutions in federal, state, and local policy (e.g., test-based accountability, increased emphases on engagement with instruction) that have changed the principal's role. Being successful as a school leader requires three different sets of abilities: teaching, working with people, and managing the school and the school community. My experience in education indicates that if these skills and expertise are manifested in the four distinct kinds of conduct discussed in the following part, four components that result in positive school effects can be generated. First, it is essential to understand that these components fall into one of the following categories: Engaging in instructional tasks with teachers. Teachers are engaged in several ways, including teacher evaluation, instructional coaching, and establishing a data-driven, school-wide instructional program to facilitate such interactions and build a productive school climate. These are forms of engagement with teachers that are centered on instructional practice. School environments are characterized by trust, efficacy, teamwork, engagement with data, and continuous improvement. They facilitate collaborative learning and professional development. To improve teacher practice and enhance student learning, teachers should work together with systems of support authentically. Strategic management of personnel and resources. Allocation of resources and staffing processes around strategic staffing.

In terms of equity, principals can impact key populations, like low-income students and students of color. The impacts can occur directly (e.g., through how they handle disciplinary actions) or indirectly (e.g., by implementing culturally responsive teaching practices with teachers, or by hiring more teachers of color who are influential for students of color). As principals of color are particularly likely to impact both students and teachers of color positively, they may have a high degree of leverage in this regard. To illuminate the approaches and strategies equity-focused principals use to affect schools serving historically marginalized student populations, we examine the growing, largely qualitative literature on leadership for equity. Furthermore, I observed that a high rate of principals leaving their schools has a detrimental effect on student progress and other outcomes, such as teacher retention and school atmosphere. Schools with enormous proportions of low-income, low-achieving, and students of color tend to have higher principal turnover rates, indicating that principal turnover can often strengthen existing inequities among schools. There have been many changes in the role of the principal, affecting the expectations about what leaders need to know, how they spend their time, and what outcomes they need to focus on. Nevertheless, there is no doubt that school leadership plays an important role in school outcomes, including the achievement of students. The importance of effective principals may have been underestimated previously-and, they may need to be stressed more in previous reports. Beyond student achievement, principals have substantive effects, focusing on instructional interactions with teachers, creating a productive school climate, fostering collaboration and professional learning communities, and managing personnel and resources strategically. To meet the needs of marginalized students, principals must develop an equity lens. These are some tactical strategies to ensure best practices are in place:

- Shaping a vision of academic success for all students
- Creating a climate hospitable to education
- Managing people, data and processes to foster school improvement
- Improving instruction and cultivating leadership in others

The importance of feedback is so obvious that it is often taken for granted during the teaching and learning process. It is a simple yet powerful tool to aid in the learning process. Feedback is any means to inform a learner of their accomplishments and areas needing improvement. There are several different forms that feedback can take. They are oral, written, computer displayed, and from any of the interactions that occur in group learning. What is important is that the learner is informed and can associate the feedback with a specific response.

GIVE PROMPT FEEDBACK

By knowing what you know and do not know gives a focus to learning. In order for students to benefit from courses, they need appropriate feedback on their performance. When starting out, students need help in evaluating their current knowledge and capabilities. Within the classroom, students need frequent opportunities to perform and receive suggestions for improvement. Throughout their time in college and especially at the end of their college career, students need chances to reflect on what they have learned, what they still need to know, and how to assess themselves.

FOR THE REGULAR CLASSROOM:

- Follow-up presentations with a five minute period for students to write down what they have learned in class.

- Provide informative comments showing the students' errors and suggestions on how they can improve.
- Discuss the results of class assignments and exams with the class and individual students.
- Vary assessment techniques (tests, papers, journaling, quizzes).
- Offer on-line testing, software simulations, and web-based programs that provide instantaneous feedback.
- Have question and answer sessions.
- Use audio and/or video recordings to assess performances.
- Return grades for assignments, projects, and tests within one week.
- For distance and online courses:
- E-mail gives instant feedback instead of waiting for the next lesson.
- Use on-line testing, software simulations, and web-based programs that provide instantaneous feedback.
- Monitor bulletin boards regularly and give specific information feedback to students.
- Use pre-class and post-class assessments.
- Schedule a chat group where you, the instructor are present. Use it as a question-and-answer session when appropriate.
- Send acknowledgment e-mails when you receive a students work.
- Post answer keys after receiving assignment from all students.
- Use of hyperlinks within text to provide feedback to questions raised within the text.

An easy assumption to make would be that students would be more successful if they spent more time studying. It makes sense, but it oversimplifies the principle of time on task. Student achievement is not simply a matter of time spent working on a task. Even though learning and development require time, it is an error to disregard how much time is available and how well the time is spent. Time on task is more complicated than one might assume.

EMPHASIZE TIME ON TASK:

Learning needs time and energy. Efficient time-management skills are critical for students. Allowing realistic amounts of time allows effective learning for students and effective teaching for faculty. The way the institution defines time expectations for students, faculty, administrators, and other staff, can create the basis for high performance from everyone.

FOR THE REGULAR CLASSROOM:

- Expect students to complete their assignments promptly.
- Clearly communicate to your students the minimum amount of time they should spend preparing for class and working on assignments.
- Help students set challenging goals for their own learning.
- Have realistic expectations (don't expect 10 papers in 10 weeks).
- Encourage students to prepare in advance for oral presentations.
- Explain to your students the consequences of non-attendance.
- Meet with students who need to catch up to discuss their study habits, schedules, and other commitments.
- Be careful that time on task is real learning, not busy work.
- Do not use technology for technology's sake. It must be relevant and useful to the topic.

- Have progressive deadlines for projects and assignments.
- Teach time management.
- Discussion topics from class posted in a discussion group on the web .
- For distance and online courses:
- Understand that there will be problems with the distance and technology along the way.
- Identify key concepts and how those will be taught. Given the amount of time, decide what realistically can be covered.
- Each distance class should involve some achievement expectation that is laid out at the beginning of the course. Assign some content for out-of-class time.
- Give up the illusion of doing it all as you might in a regular classroom.
- Vary the types of interaction. In creating an interactive environment, it can be overwhelming to the students and teacher if the types of interaction required are too time-consuming.
- Consider both in and out of class time.
- Ensure you know your goals and that the learners understand them as well.
- Have regular discussions that require participation.

2ND QUARTER

CONTINUE THE **IMPLEMENTATION** OF YOUR INITIAL GAME PLAN.

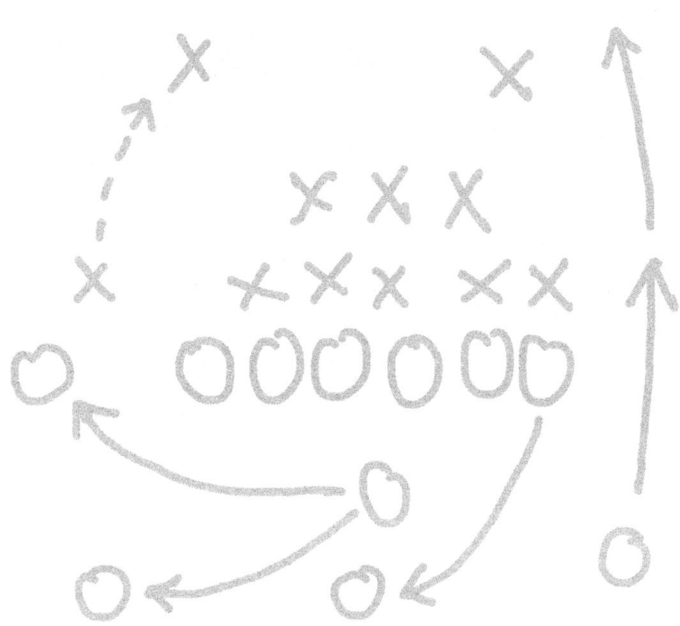

2ND QUARTER

Continue the IMPLEMENTATION of your initial game plan.

Execution is critical to ensure that you are moving forward, onward, and upward towards victory. Administrators all have the same goal at the end of the day: improving schools, right? Creating action steps based on a school improvement plan makes perfect sense. Describe goals, strategies, and actions aimed at improving the quality of education students receive at their schools according to the state's requirements included in school improvement plans—the first step. Make your text more engaging and easier to understand using more active voice and concise language. Rather than writing, "All administrators aim to improve schools, right?" note, "Administrators aim to improve schools."

Second step. Provide specific examples or case studies to demonstrate how a school improvement plan can be implemented successfully. Again, it can help readers understand the benefits of having a SIP and how to apply it.

Third step. Provide more information about how teachers, students, and parents can participate in the school improvement plan. School improvement plan goals are typically aligned to outcomes on statewide assessments, which can lead to a sense of ownership and shared responsibility for the school's success. This can make the plan more effective. For the school improvement plans to work, all building-level employees must be aware of the school's improvement plan and, in return, will be more likely to believe in its effectiveness.

Usually, the principal is responsible for implementing the action steps outlined in an improvement plan. Generally, the school's principal takes responsibility for all the steps outlined in the improvement plan and executes them.

Similarly, the principal might delegate specific tasks without taking responsibility for the larger goal. Implementing the school improvement plan does not have to be - or should not be - a time-consuming and draining process.

The big question is: What makes an effective school improvement plan?

Improvement, documented processes, regular leadership inspection, and feedback on goals progress.

FIVE CRITICAL STRATEGIES MISSING FROM MOST SCHOOL IMPROVEMENT PLAN GOALS:

- Distributed responsibilities
- Weekly metrics
- Sustainable systems with documented processes
- Classroom walks & feedback.
- Continuous improvement meetings

1. Distribute responsibilities to others rather than being a hero leader

The school principal, teachers, and other education professionals stand in a circle with their hands together, representing teamwork and distributed leadership responsibilities. Distributed system maturity begins with shifting from a "hero leader" to empowering your team to take some ownership of school improvement goals.

Hero leadership means that a leader takes on responsibilities alone. Therefore, it is not a system for genuine school improvement because it heavily relies on one individual.

Are there any "hero" principals that come to mind when thinking of heroes? School leaders that work long hours to lead improvement in our schools is heartbreaking. Nothing is more heart-wrenching than considering what these men and women sacrifice for their families and the damage they do to their mental and physical health due to what they do. There is a need to change that as soon as possible!

To start implementing distributed leadership, what do you need to do?

There is no doubt that school improvement plans must include at least the individuals responsible for each step of each objective to succeed. It is essential to leave the task management of these action steps in the hands of those responsible for implementing them. Preparation for the new school year should begin months before the school year begins to ensure it is successful.

2. Use metrics to monitor every week rather than bi-annually

A principal or educator looks at charts and graphs on his computer monitoring progress toward a school improvement plan goal. Don't stop there! What would it look like if you added a goal for improvement tied to a metric for progress monitoring?

3. Develop sustainable systems with documented processes rather than relying on the talents of individuals.

4. Provide regular inspections of classrooms and feedback on the progress that has been made toward the goal

Closeup of someone holding a pen and writing on a clipboard representing a school principal. This is providing feedback on progress toward the school improvement plan goal. I can imagine you asking: In all of this, where is the principal? It is the individual's responsibility to ensure that the goal is achieved. Without a doubt! The principal's role is crucial in a model of distributed system maturity. They are responsible for regular leadership inspections and feedback on the system's progress. In our experience, when the principal takes these two responsibilities and focuses on them, the results are most reliable, the risk of failure is the lowest, and the highest ownership levels are achieved. As a result of this, system performance goals can be achieved. I suggest you reflect on all the research and discussions over the years. These discussions pertain to the importance of the principal being the school's instructional leader.

5. Ensure continuous improvement for your team through daily stand-ups

A school principal stands before an active board with two teachers or educators during a daily stand-up. This is to review progress toward school improvement plan goals. The final strategy that combines the distributed system maturity model is regular feedback on the team's progress and efficacy in meeting school improvement plan goals.

This critical process belongs to the principal as with leadership inspection of action steps.

At the heart of continuous improvement is the daily stand-up. A daily stand-up is when SLT members gather around the action board as the principal leads 10 to 20 minutes of discussion. The daily stand-up takes place at the same time and location every day.

This time is sacred.

It would be best if you considered when the daily stand-up should occur. Support staff should know and protect this time.

During the daily stand-up, the principal asks each SLT member what they observed the previous day, moving us toward meeting our definition of done.

In other words, this document is not meant to summarize what each student did or did not do in the classroom. Instead, it focuses on specific classroom actions and outcomes that contributed to achieving the defined goal. Aside from that, it's now time to find out if there are any challenges to meeting the plan for the week.

Data is central to all discussions. The game plan for tomorrow is also cemented—no more yearly, quarterly, monthly, or weekly focus on where we are as a school. Now you know daily!

The SLT will likely have other purposes and other members responsible for implementing the goals (such as the core subject areas and SEL personnel coaches).

What results can you expect after using the five strategies?

Using these five strategies in full, what should a school look like?

(Coaching Points) HONOR TEACHERS

It's essential to understand the concerns of the teachers. Some have been through various leaders and reforms, so they may need more time to trust new leadership. To gain their trust and demonstrate their insights are valued, ask them two questions: "What concerns do you have about the school?" and "What must be honored?" It's best to do this over the summer when possible and take notes to ensure you understand their perspectives. Then, try to delve deeper into their responses for a better understanding. At a meeting held in the early stages of the faculty's operations., you should summarize the various conversations you've had with staff and ask them if what you heard resonates with them. This will lead to rich discussions. Listening attentively to verbal and nonverbal cues during these conversations is essential. The agenda for the meeting should be based on the staff's concerns and hopes. In this way, the conference will indeed be a collaborative effort. Your staff's collective wisdom is an invaluable asset. You must approach them respectfully and utilize their knowledge, demonstrating that you value and acknowledge their expertise. This will showcase your eagerness to learn from them and ensure their contributions are recognized and appreciated.

YOUR THOUGHTS:

PRINCIPLE III.

CHANGE: If nothing changes, then nothing changes

CORE BELIEF

To succeed here, students must develop social and emotional skills, including cooperation, assertiveness, responsibility, empathy, and self-control—and academic competencies—academic mindset, perseverance, learning strategies, and behaviors.

GUIDING PRINCIPLES

Education theorists' work and classroom teachers' experiences inform the Responsive Classroom approach. Six principles guide this approach:

- As important as teaching academic content is teaching social and emotional skills.
- In addition to what we teach, how we teach is equally essential.
- Significant cognitive growth occurs through social interaction.
- As adults, it is essential to work together to create a safe, joyful, and inclusive school environment.

Our knowledge and beliefs about our students- individually, culturally, and developmentally—inform our expectations, reactions, and attitudes about those students.

Knowing our students is just as important as knowing them in partnering with families and valuing their contributions.

STRATEGIES AND PRACTICES IN THE CLASSROOM

It is based on the belief that students learn best when academic and social-emotional skills are integrated. Academic and social-emotional competencies are developed through the Responsive Classroom approach. Teachers can gradually introduce this approach into their practice with many different programs where students can do their best learning.

In the Responsive Classroom, these core practices are essential:

SHARED PRACTICES

Using interactive modeling to teach procedures and routines (such as entering and exiting the room and engaging with text) are examples of academic and social skills in giving and receiving feedback.

It is the intentional use of language by teachers to engage students in their learning and to develop their academic, social, and emotional skills.

Teachers can set clear limits, and students can maintain dignity while fixing and learning from their mistakes with logical consequences.

Active (hands-on) and interactive (social) learning structures—Activities that engage students with content in a dynamic (hands-on) and interactive manner.

Morning Meeting—Everyone In the classroom, students gather in a circle for twenty to thirty minutes daily to participate in four sequential activities: greeting, sharing, group activity, and morning message.

Establishing Rules—The teacher and students work together to develop rules that will help everyone achieve their individual goals for the year and help the teacher and students reach those goals together in the future.

Energizers—Short, playful, whole-group activities used as lesson breaks.

Following lunch and recess, a brief, purposeful, and relaxed transition time takes place before the rest of the school day begins.

Participation in a brief activity or two promotes reflection and celebration.

Responsive Advisory Meeting—Develop meaningful connections while developing respectful, trusting relationships with students through a predictable routine based on one of seven distinct purposes.

Investing Students in the Rules—A process facilitated by the teacher composed of four steps:

- Setting SMART goals.
- Connecting the destinations to rules.
- Relating the rules to concrete behaviors.
- Making the traditions come alive.

Brain Breaks—Short breaks in whole-class lessons that allow students to move and interact, used to increase focus, motivation, learning, and memory.

Active Teaching—A strategy for delivering curriculum content where the teacher presents, explains, illustrates, and demonstrates the scope of the learning objective is met by students in this way. A method of active teaching consists of three phases: Teach and Model, Student Collaboration, and Facilitated Reflection.

Student Practice—A process that follows active teaching where students explore and practice the content and skills taught during a lesson under the teacher's guidance. This allows the teacher to identify and correct students' thinking before they practice independently.

Small Group Learning—A teacher-organized getting students to work together on a task, project, or goal is part of the learning process.

So far, the previous passage has described one Character, a "Turnaround Leader."

One primary reason for turnaround school success is strong transformational leadership from principals on campus. But what determines an effective leader from an ineffective one? First, look at the qualities that make for a strong turnaround leader, as specified in Public Impact's cross-sector research.

1. Results-Driven

A significant characteristic of a successful turnaround principal is their ability to focus on task-oriented actions that lead to measurable results. In addition, their drive to achieve challenging goals despite their setbacks is crucial in reaching a high-performance standard.

The transformational leader's planning for the future helps them identify potential problems and ways to combat them. As part of the implementation plan, the principal should also set clear expectations for staff and hold them accountable. This ensures that everyone understands the goal and the steps needed to reach it.

Finally, a results-driven leader shows initiative and perseverance in executing the plan.

2. Motivational

Another characteristic of an effective turnaround leader is motivating others to get results. A principal knows that they cannot bring about change on their campus alone and that it takes a network of people to achieve a goal. Therefore, they need to be authoritative leaders who work with and through others on their team.

In addition, they emphasize developing others. They leverage relationships to increase the short-term and long-term effectiveness of their staff. A turnaround leader ensures they are equipping others for the task and building them up for the future.

3. Problem-Solver

To turn around campus effectively, a principal must think critically and attack issues with a problem-solving mentality. As part of the problem-solving process, they should analyze relevant data, make clear plans to attack the problem, and ensure that classroom activities align with the school's overall learning goals.

In addition, the turnaround leader must use analytical and conceptual thinking to simplify complex problems. By recognizing cause and effect and patterns among seemingly unrelated things, the principal can develop new solutions to issues that may have plagued the school.

4. Self-confident

Finally, an essential characteristic of a turnaround leader is the ability to lead confidently. This may be one of the more complex qualities to deliver consistently. However, an outward display of faith by staying focused, committed, and self-assured can go a long way in leading staff. Transformational leaders know their work is essential but challenging, so they remain resolved despite setbacks and personal/professional attacks.

After discussing the characteristics of an effective turnaround leader, let's discuss how to develop these skills further. You can start by identifying your strengths and growth areas through self-assessment and colleague feedback. If you know where you are, it can be challenging to pinpoint how you're growing. One way to do this is through the Turnaround Leader 360 Feedback Assessment. This mobile-ready online survey collects anonymous feedback from peers, your supervisor, and staff. It gives insight into your research-based turnaround leader actions and turnaround leader competencies. Once you have insight into your leadership actions and competencies, use that information to craft personalized development goals. Then, work backward to identify action steps to meet those goals. Your willingness to continue to develop as an effective turnaround leader will make all the difference on your campus. Now in changing things, you also have to change something that will affect the climate and culture of your school!

Craft a compelling reward program. When creating a PBIS rewards program for your students, remember to make an equally effective reward program for your teachers. It is important to note that in the case of PBIS used by teachers, it is governed by the teacher's Individualized Education

Plan! Business owners appreciate teachers' work, so getting them on board is easier than you think. Do their jobs better and happier, but grabbing some advocating rewards along the way adds to their motivation. Likewise, do their jobs better and more comfortably; scooping up some advocating tips along the way is an additional motivator. Plus, it's fun! Try recruiting local businesses to help by donating prizes or offering your school and staff discounted prices. Business owners appreciate teachers' work, so getting them on board is much easier than you think. Teachers' work, so getting them on board is far easier than you might realize.

5. Recognize (and reward) effort.

As well as recognizing tangible achievements, acknowledge teachers' measures. This is especially true when implementing a PBIS initiative; there must be more clarity, resistance, or friction in getting it up and running. You reassure your teachers that they are progressing when you acknowledge their efforts. Participation in PBIS will also increase teachers' likelihood of adopting it.

6. Ask for their opinions.

Ask for your teachers' input when putting something together — a special event or an upcoming initiative. They'll feel a greater sense of ownership of the idea. They may have suggestions you hadn't even thought of that could make bringing upcoming initiatives and special events to fruition easier.

7. Please allow them to express themselves.

Could you share teachers' thoughts by creating a forum? You'll unearth some real gems the school can benefit from, even if not all are workable. It is often the mere fact that you are open to their ideas that is a huge motivator for some teachers, particularly those more proactive in their approach.

8. Recognize them when they're busy or stressed.

Show extra appreciation when teachers are particularly busy or stressed, do something as simple as voicing that you know they're engaged, and appreciate their effort and work. It may not be much, but it shows empathy and gratitude. Also, please waive or shorten meetings during these busy periods.

9. Put exciting events on the calendar throughout the year.

Although sporting events and after-school activities are fun for students and parents, they can be extra work for the staff. But, of course, for many teachers, The joy it brings to their students makes them happy to do it, So why not sweeten the deal by planning something exciting for them afterward? For example, serve a celebratory spread in the teacher's lounge after an event!

10. Buy them lunch.

Why not buy your staff lunch periodically, like once a month or semester? Please inform them beforehand so those who usually pack lunch won't have to fill it that day. Also, please note any allergies or food restrictions ahead of time.

11. The morning/afternoon off voucher

Give every teacher a coupon for a fuss-free morning or afternoon off every semester. All they need to do is give some notice to arrange a substitute. The fact that they keep that voucher in their back pocket is reassuring to them as they know they have an out in case they are overwhelmed or if something unexpected happens. As a bonus, it is another tiny gesture showing how much you care about their actions.

12. Free coffee/snacks

Occasionally, provide complimentary coffee and tea in the teacher's lounge for staff to enjoy on their breaks or some healthy snacks, like a fruit tray, so that teachers can recognize each other's hard work.

Recognizing your teachers is essential, but creating ways for them to recognize each other is lovely. You could also expand this idea to allow parents and students to share their appreciation. Here's a simple concept: Give people cards to write thank you notes and a box to drop them in letters. Please create an inbox for gratitude messages.

Once a month, share recognition and appreciation for individual teachers in a meeting or schoolwide communications. Highlighting the school's positive aspects will send a powerful message to your teachers.

(Coaching Point) DON'T CHANGE EVERYTHING

In the early stages of your role, it's best only to make necessary alterations if instructed by your superintendent or school board. However, feel free to add a personal touch to your office by swapping out the pictures on your wall. As a newcomer, your primary focus should be on learning the ropes. While it's great to have big plans for improving the school, it's essential to recognize that implementing significant changes should be something other than your top priority.

Even the most unexpected aspects of a school's culture can hold symbolic significance. While a new leader may have good intentions, mending any damage can prove challenging. Although enhancing the school is an important goal, it is crucial to identify potential obstacles before initiating any changes. Before diving in, take the time to familiarize yourself with any pitfalls or potential threats.

YOUR THOUGHTS: ____________________

PRINCIPLE IV

Keep a bird's eye view of the pulse of your school by making DATA-DRIVEN DECISIONS to justify your next moves.

In education, the concept of relying on intuition or gut feelings to determine right or wrong is widely recognized. However, data-driven decisions are becoming increasingly popular. This approach involves continuously assessing student learning, analyzing assessment data, and intentionally adjusting instruction based on that data in cycles, such as daily or weekly. In education, principals use data in various ways to make decisions. They incorporate it into their reflective teaching practices by observing, drawing inferences, and adjusting their leadership styles on a daily basis. At times, adjustments are made on the spot, such as when a principal observes a teacher providing customized reading material to a student who needs extra support in reading. Other times, long-term changes in instructional methods may be necessary to accommodate the needs of some students. In such cases, the principal provides feedback to the teacher, who then integrates it into their teaching practices.

Schools use collaboration to analyze data effectively. This includes studying standardized test scores, attendance, and behavior data to make informed decisions for the betterment of their schools. Using data, educators can identify students who may need extra support, recognize gaps in the curriculum, and align curriculums across departments and grades. Encouraging a collaborative approach to data among teachers fosters shared responsibility and helps them view their instruction as a crucial part of a more significant effort to serve students better. To make the most of data, administrators, and teachers should consider the following tips: principals should review past data to establish a baseline understanding of their students. Analyzing past data can provide valuable insights for teachers regarding the skills their students have mastered and areas where they may need additional support. For example, educators can use standardized tests to determine a student's level of advancement - whether they are advanced, proficient, essential, or below basic. This can help them comprehend why certain classes are moving slower than others. This information can also assist teachers in creating customized accommodations for students who require extra assistance. For example, teachers can seat students at the below-basic level in the front of the classroom for easy access to additional support.

Additionally, advanced students can be provided alternative activities that offer them a more significant challenge. Principals should evaluate student performance using a variety of data types. Data obtained solely from an end-of-unit exam miss valuable information about students' strengths, weaknesses, and preferences. Simple formative assessments, such as thumbs-up/thumbs-down check-ins, can help teachers gauge student comprehension and engagement quickly. Observing students' interpersonal and social successes can provide teachers with insights into which activities students enjoy and with whom they work best. This is valuable information when grouping students for collaborative work or lesson planning.

As a principal, it is crucial to grasp the significance of relevant data when addressing specific inquiries. For example, although data concerning a cluster of underprivileged students can glimpse their overall academic struggles, it might not explain why a particular student fared poorly in an exam. Acknowledging data limitations enables teachers to diagnose problems more precisely and respond with effective interventions. Conversely, depending exclusively on background information to account for poor performance may result in disregarding underlying issues.

REMAIN VIGILANT AND WATCHFUL FOR ANY UNANTICIPATED TRENDS THAT MAY EMERGE

Student success can be influenced by factors beyond a principal's control, such as the responsibility of getting younger siblings ready for school. This can cause students to arrive late to class and miss quizzes. However, when principals and teachers know these issues, they can find ways to assist students. For example, instead of denying students the chance to make up missed quizzes, teachers can make accommodations to help them. By asking simple questions like "Why are you consistently late?" teachers can acquire the necessary information to personalize their approach.

Additionally, attentive principals and teachers are vigilant in observing student behavior and performance trends. For instance, while reviewing test scores over the past few months, some faculty members may discover that students perform better on Mondays than Fridays. Upon questioning the students, they may learn that math tests are always scheduled on Fridays, resulting in students having to study for two tests the night before, ultimately reducing their preparation time. Armed with this information, the principal and staff can collaborate with their colleagues to schedule exam days more efficiently.

UTILIZE A RANGE OF DATA TOOLS.

With the new technology available today, educators can easily make data-driven decisions. These tools, many of which are free, enable teachers to uncover hidden patterns and insights or organize and make data accessible for analysis. Electronic grade books offer added features, such as individual and class statistics, the ability to attach standards to assignments, and analysis of student accomplishments, replacing traditional grade books as the primary tool for record-keeping. In addition, programs like Edulastic and Flipgrid provide formative assessments and instant feedback on student learning, allowing teachers to check in with students throughout the class and confidently grade low-stakes assessments like exit tickets.

CREATE NEW LESSON PLANS BASED ON DATA

Educators can use various data types to help them plan their lessons effectively. For example, they need to consider their students' skill gaps, the number of students who have a basic, proficient, or below-basic understanding of the subject, and their student's interests. Teachers can survey their students at the start of the academic year and during the term to discover their favorite topics and activities. With this information, teachers can create lessons that concentrate on the subjects their students enjoy the most and include their preferred learning methods in the curriculum.

LEARN HOW TO ENHANCE STUDENT PERFORMANCE BY UTILIZING DATA

Analysis of the right data allows teachers to identify contributors to student success and failure. Once those contributors are located, teachers can devise solutions to address them. For example, by analyzing a struggling student's homework grades and test scores, a teacher may gather important insights about where a deficiency in understanding exists or, perhaps, which question formats pose challenges. Once such discoveries are made, a teacher can design exercises and activities for students in their trouble areas that help improve their performance.

IT'S RECOMMENDED TO UTILIZE VARIOUS DATA SOURCES FOR BETTER INSIGHTS

To make informed decisions about their instruction, educators should use various data sources and communicate with their colleagues regularly. These data sources include student writing samples, group projects, homework, test grades, student surveys, and reflections on their learning. By analyzing this data, teachers can determine which skills to incorporate into their lesson plans, which texts and materials to use, and which activities to include.

For example, a science teacher creating a new curriculum may review previous homework reports and find that students needed help understanding the functions of cell parts. As a result, the teacher includes lessons that cover cell functions. After reading students' end-of-unit reflections, the teacher realizes that students found visual models helpful. Therefore, the new unit incorporates more visual models to explain concepts. Ultimately, the teacher revises their instruction based on the data they collected. Collecting data from multiple sources can provide educators with valuable insights that can be utilized to design impactful coursework for their students.

IT'S IMPORTANT TO KNOW WHEN DATA MIGHT NOT BE APPROPRIATE

Educators need to remember that not all data analysis can be applied universally. Even when situations seem similar, there may be underlying factors that can lead to different outcomes. For instance, a freshman English teacher may analyze data showing how a new peer-editing method improved student essays in a colleague's sophomore English class. However, assuming that implementing the same method in the freshman class will also lead to improvement may be short-sighted. There could be factors like the analytical skills of the ninth-graders or the lack of advanced students to lead the activity that could impact the results. Educators should consider factors such as class structure, size, age, and background to interpret data and understand their impact on student learning.

CREATE DATA VISUALIZATIONS.

Educators sometimes need to exchange data to help understand trends within their school. To make this data more accessible, they can use visual models such as pie charts, graphs, or PowerPoint presentations. By selecting relevant data points, they can showcase how students are performing in different subject areas and help colleagues teaching the same grade level or subject gain insights into student strengths and weaknesses. This can be especially helpful for department teams when analyzing incoming students. The ongoing development of data and analytics can bring advantages to principals, teachers, and students. Teachers can integrate data-based teaching methods into their work and utilize new tools to work more efficiently and enhance student performance. To help educators create solutions that provide equal opportunities for marginalized students, it is crucial to learn how to leverage data and gain a thorough understanding of the intricate social justice issues that students encounter.

(PCH Coaching Point) TIME MANAGEMENT

Effective time management is a crucial skill frequently discussed but not constantly scrutinized. For example, you may have heard the phrase, "My door is always open," which implies that a leader should always be available. However, this can go against the fundamental principles of sound time management.

Principals need to have control over their time. Keeping your door open can lead to interruptions and a loss of control. On the other hand, closing the door can prevent unexpected visitors from disrupting your work. It's best to complete office work outside of school hours when there are fewer disturbances, which can ensure accuracy and coherence in paperwork.

To appear friendly and accessible, stepping out of the office and visiting the school while it's in session is essential. As a principal, it's crucial to interact with students and staff and observe instruction daily. However, new principals should remember to set digital and physical boundaries. Being too accessible can negatively impact personal relationships and health. Principals must manage their availability, especially regarding text messages, voicemails, and emails. Although they can be available 24/7, taking breaks and going home at a reasonable hour is essential. Of course, personal phone numbers should be available to key personnel in case of emergencies. Superintendents should remind principals to prioritize their well-being and disconnect from technology when necessary.

YOUR THOUGHTS:

HALFTIME

AS A PRINCIPAL, YOU MUST DECIDE WHICH WAY YOU MUST GO.

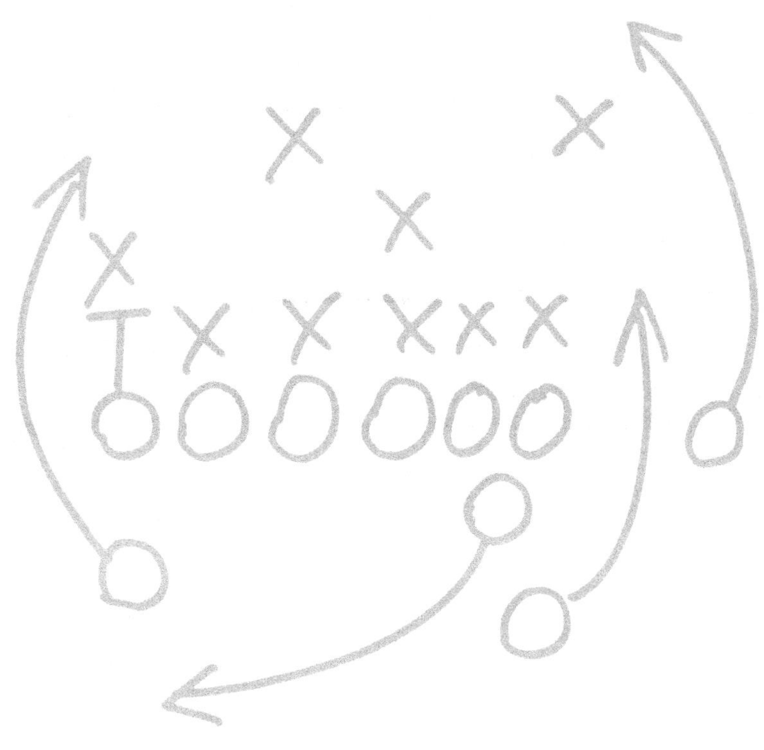

HALFTIME

As a principal, you must decide which way you must go.

Lets utilize this break to make some ***ADJUSTMENTS*** and remember the game plan, vision, and the outcomes you want. Assess what›s working and what›s not.

Just like in sports, players and coaches spend the off-season getting into shape. This is needed to be at peak performance during the season.

However, as principals, how often do we spend the summertime getting our faculty and staff into school shape? First, sports coaches develop a clear philosophy and vision for their programs. Then, collaborating with the sport program directors, they develop, implement, and manage the program's goals. Principals should take the same approach as they can craft their vision for their school and community similarly.

To meet this responsibility, principals must:

____

____

____

____

____

____

HALFTIME ADJUSTMENT #1

Develop and enact an athlete-centered coaching philosophy.

Focusing on faculty and staff development, principals prioritize opportunities for growth over winning at all costs. Principals must provide opportunities for faculty and staff to reach their full potential within their respective areas.

To meet this responsibility, principals must:

____

____

____

____

____

____

HALFTIME ADJUSTMENT #2

Use long-term staff development to develop potential, enhance literacy, and encourage lifelong career activity.

Principals understand and implement developmentally appropriate principles associated with long-term teachers.

To meet this responsibility, principals must:

____

____

____

____

____

____

HALFTIME ADJUSTMENT #3

Using strategic planning and goal-setting principles, create a unified vision. Principals must set and achieve goals for students, faculty, staff, and stakeholders to develop physically, behaviorally, and socially. The plans are aligned with the school vision, school district philosophy, and the long-term development of everyone involved.

To meet this responsibility, principals must:

____

____

____

____

____

____

HALFTIME ADJUSTMENT #4

Align the program with all rules and regulations and the needs of the school and school community.

Sports coaches adhere to national, regional, local, and institutional guidelines and regulations to ensure the program complies. Principals also align the program with the community's needs and individual faculty and staff.

To meet this responsibility, principals must:

____

____

____

____

____

HALFTIME ADJUSTMENT #5

Responsibly manage program resources.

Program documents are managed by principals, who possess fundamental fiscal and facility management knowledge tailored to their program.

To meet this responsibility, principals must:

____

____

____

____

____

____

HALFTIME ADJUSTMENT #6

Engage in and Support Ethical Practices

Sports coaches know the significance of ethical practices. Therefore, they follow ethical behavior and adhere to codes of conduct related to their sport and coaching environment. They also instruct their sports programs on ethical conduct.

To meet this responsibility, principals must:

____

____

____

____

____

____

HALFTIME ADJUSTMENT #7

Build Relationships

Coaches in sports develop competencies for communicating, collaborating, educating, and supporting all stakeholders involved in the sports program (athletes, administrators, assistant coaches, support staff, referees, sports medicine professionals, program supporters, parents, and media). It is the responsibility of principals to fulfill this responsibility by:

To meet this responsibility, principals must:

____

____

____

____

____

____

HALFTIME ADJUSTMENT #8

Develop a Safe Sport Environment

Sports coaches can establish a secure and supportive environment for athletes by adhering to the guidelines provided by sports organizations, coaching science, and state and federal laws.

To meet this responsibility, principals must:

____

____

____

____

____

HALFTIME ADJUSTMENT #9

Create a Positive and Inclusive Sport Environment

Sports coaches create practice plans that aim to enhance the overall well-being of their athletes, both physically and mentally. Their season plans prioritize positive outcomes and encourage sports participation to benefit the athletes' physical, psychological, and social health. In addition, sports coaches implement strategies to promote the participation of all athletes.

To meet this responsibility, principals must:

____

____

____

____

HALFTIME ADJUSTMENT #10

Conduct Practices and Prepare for the Competition

Sports coaches utilize coaching science, sport-specific knowledge, and best practices to conduct high-quality sports practices, prepare athletes for competition, and manage contests effectively. The approach centers around how coaches plan, teach, assess, and adapt in practices and competitions. Principals must manage extra-curricular activites as well as the school day.

To meet this responsibility, principals must:

____

____

____

____

HALFTIME ADJUSTMENT #11

Strive for Continuous Improvement

Principals continually improve through self-reflection, mentorship, professional development, evaluation, and self-care.

To meet this responsibility, principals must:

____

____

____

____

____

____

(Pch Coaching Point) PICK YOUR BATTLES

When I became principal, cell phones were not allowed in school. Teachers would keep track of students who broke this rule, and after three offenses, the student would be reported to the assistant principal. Parents were contacted if the issue persisted. However, we eventually decided to focus on topics related to teaching and learning, and the cell phone battle gradually became less important. Our district even created a program called B.Y.O.D (Bring Your Own Device), which allowed students to use their cell phones during technology-based lessons. It's important to recognize which battles are worth fighting and which are not, and to prioritize topics that have a direct impact on education. Where we choose to devote our time reflects our values.

YOUR THOUGHTS:

3RD QUARTER

IT'S TIME TO TAKE THE **LEAD**; IF YOU HAVEN'T REALIZED IT, YOU DETERMINE WHETHER YOUR SCHOOL FAILS OR SUCCEEDS.

3RD QUARTER

It's time to take the LEAD; if you haven't realized it, you determine whether your school fails or succeeds.

Often we as school leaders must stop and adjust the type of leadership we govern ourselves and the leadership style we want others to see.

TRANSFORMATIONAL LEADERSHIP

The name of this leadership style says it all - Transformational leaders aim to inspire their employees to innovate and bring positive changes to the businesses or groups they lead.

These leaders strive to improve and discover more efficient ways to accomplish tasks. Their actions inspire and encourage others to take ownership of their work and contribute suggestions or observations on optimizing things. Under the guidance of transformational leaders, individuals are granted significant autonomy and ample space to innovate and explore unconventional ideas.

Pro: *Leaders can successfully unite their employees towards a shared vision or goal by establishing and nurturing trust.*

Con: *It's common to face resistance when trying to implement changes in environments where people are attached to the current way of doing things.*

You Might Be a Transformational Leader If...

You possess a perceptive ability to identify areas for improvement and maintain an optimistic outlook that any process can be optimized.

You have a remarkable ability to motivate others to step outside their comfort zones and exceed their limits. It brings you great joy and pride to witness team members accomplishing things they once deemed impossible.

DEMOCRATIC LEADERSHIP

This type of leadership is often referred to as "participative leadership." These leaders democratically operate their teams and projects, even if they hold higher positions in the organizational hierarchy. They strongly emphasize collaboration and actively involve their team members in decision-making. Leaders with a democratic style place great importance on the opinions and suggestions of others, and they promote open dialogue to discuss such contributions. Rather than dictating instructions from a position of authority, they adopt a more cooperative approach to achieving objectives.

Pro: *Encouraging creativity and promoting innovation at work can positively affect the happiness and satisfaction of your employees and team members.*

Con: *Attempting to reach a group consensus can often result in inefficiency and potentially high costs.*

You Might Be a Democratic Leader If...

- The best meetings are where everyone can weigh in equally.
- You can only remember the last time you made an important decision by getting input from at least one other person.

BUREAUCRATIC LEADERSHIP

The bureaucratic leadership style is characterized by rigorous adherence to rules and procedures that must be followed to achieve effectiveness as a leader.

One example of leadership is bureaucratic leadership, where individuals hold power based on their formal position or title rather than personal qualities.

To effectively manage others and make decisions, those in leadership positions must adhere to a predetermined set of responsibilities, rules, and systems. Therefore, they need to follow the established roadmap.

Pro: *The systematic nature of this leadership approach provides remarkable stability, even when faced with personnel changes or other potential disruptions. Consistency remains a steadfast feature of operations.*

Con: *It can be tempting to stick to old ways of doing things just because that›s how it›s always been done. However, this approach can limit flexibility and creativity among employees, and it›s essential to make room for new ideas.*

You Might Be a Bureaucratic Leader If...

- It's common for you to wonder how your predecessor would handle certain situations. You want to ensure that you're adhering to the correct procedure. Whenever you're assigned a new task, you always seek confirmation that you're doing it correctly.

CHARISMATIC LEADERSHIP

You recognize the significance of charisma, a trait many influential leaders possess. Charismatic individuals have a powerful presence and exhibit unwavering determination toward their goals.

Instead of imposing strict instructions, these leaders inspire their teams through effective communication and persuasion. They articulate their vision, rallying their team around a common goal and motivating them to work towards it.

Pro: *Charismatic leaders have the power to encourage and rally a group of people toward a common goal with practical and efficient methods.*

Con: *These leaders can be so focused that they may develop "tunnel vision" and overlook other crucial issues or tasks that arise.*

You Might Be a Charismatic Leader If...

You have a reputation for delivering outstanding motivational speeches that inspire and motivate the audience. As a result, your colleagues often choose you to give lectures and toasts at various company gatherings.

LAISSEZ-FAIRE LEADERSHIP

Do you remember "laissez-faire" from your French or history class? If not, let's refresh your memory.

The leadership approach of "laissez-faire," a French term meaning "leave it be," involves minimal intervention and stands in contrast to micromanagement.

Leaders who adopt a laissez-faire approach offer their team members the required tools and resources. They then step back and allow team members to make decisions, solve problems, and complete their tasks without constant monitoring or supervision from the leader.

Pro: *Giving teams the freedom to be creative and self-motivated is empowering and builds trust.*

Con: *When a team is disorganized or lacks self-direction, chaos, and confusion are inevitable.*

You Might Be a Laissez-Faire Leader If...

To enhance communication during project status update meetings, increasing your vocal contributions and allowing team members to provide updates would be beneficial. Your involvement in tasks and projects is mainly limited to the initial and final stages.

AUTOCRATIC LEADERSHIP

Autocratic leadership represents a stark contrast to democratic leadership. It is characterized by a "my way or the highway" mentality, wherein leaders wield complete authority and dictate decisions for their team members. They are responsible for outlining what must be accomplished and dictating how it should be done.

Pro: *Efficient and effective teams rely on swift and calculated decision-making to stay on course.*

Con: *At times, employees can experience a sense of being ignored, constrained, or unfairly treated.*

You Might Be an Autocratic Leader If:

- You believe making essential decisions alone is more efficient than group discussions and brainstorming sessions.
- It bothers you when your employees question your decisions, especially when you've already made a final decision.

SERVANT LEADERSHIP

The guiding principle of servant leaders is to prioritize serving others before leading them.

Their utmost focus is serving others relentlessly rather than attempting to sway or inspire them. They relentlessly devote their energies to finding ways to aid others and always put the needs of others before their own.

Although they possess natural leadership abilities, those who adopt the servant leadership approach do not cling to their status or power. Instead, they prioritize the growth and advancement of those who follow them.

True leaders are those who selflessly sacrifice their own time, energy, money, and even food for the sake of others. They always prioritize the needs of their team and choose to put them first, even if it means eating last.

Pro: *Implementing this approach can enhance employee morale, foster trust, and ultimately lead to improved performance and more favorable company culture.*

Con: *It can be difficult to constantly prioritize others and neglect our own needs, which is something that only comes naturally to some people.*

You Might Be a Servant Leader If...

You are recognized for frequently asking, "How can I assist?" throughout the day. Your primary focus is eliminating obstacles and supporting others in accomplishing their tasks.

You willingly offer your help when requested, knowing that your list of tasks will still await you when you return.

TRANSACTIONAL LEADERSHIP

Transactional leadership can be viewed as a straightforward transactional process where the leader issues clear instructions to their team and utilizes incentives or consequences to acknowledge or adjust their performance. For instance, a team member who accomplishes a task well may receive praise from their leader, while an undesirable task may be assigned to them if they miss a deadline. These are common ways to employ rewards and punishments in a work setting.

It is crucial to highlight that this method is highly authoritative and widely recognized as a "telling" leadership style.

Pro: *Confusion and guesswork are eliminated because the leader maps out tasks and expectations.*

Con: *Strict environments and high expectations may hinder creativity and innovation.*

You Might Be a Transactional Leader If...

- To encourage your team, you often threaten to make them stay late.
- You always come up with creative ideas to acknowledge good work, and your team is excited to see what you have in store after the successful teacher PBIS celebration last month.

COERCIVE LEADERSHIP STYLE | THE BOSS

The management style of a coercive leader is based on the principle of "Do what I say." They lead their team in a way that resembles a sergeant leading their troops into battle, demonstrating great initiative and self-discipline.

Coercive leaders often adopt a style closely associated with the armed forces.:

- Request immediate compliance.

- Be able to handle crises effectively.

- Encourage change and motivation.

- Address employees who exhibit problematic behavior.

Remembering this leadership style can harm creative individuals and projects is important. While some followers may feel secure and supported, highly skilled employees may become demotivated and resentful of excessive control.

It is highly advisable to build trust and earn the admiration of your staff by embracing adaptable work arrangements or adopting a growth mindset.

AUTHORITATIVE LEADERSHIP STYLE | THE VISIONARY

This leader is an excellent example of the authoritative leadership style described by Goleman's theory. In addition, they are an innovative and daring educator who inspires the organization with a convincing "follow me" approach to achieve our ultimate goals.

This leadership style is characterized by self-confidence, emotional intelligence, and the ability to empathize with others. In addition, they exude charisma and are adept at expressing their ideas clearly and passionately.

AFFILIATIVE LEADERSHIP STYLE | THE CARER

We are now discussing a leadership approach that emphasizes emotional connection and prioritizes creating a positive work environment. This is known as an affiliative leadership style.

The affiliative leadership style requires empathy and building relationships through various communication styles.

Using this approach can be especially beneficial in challenging situations. When implemented effectively, it can inspire employees to persevere through adversity, mend broken relationships, or form new teams.

On the flip side, this leader can need help understanding how to improve poor performance and may be more hesitant to provide advice.

DEMOCRATIC LEADERSHIP STYLE | THE LISTENER

Leaders who practice the democratic leadership style often ask for input from their team by asking, "So, what do you think?" They prioritize collaboration and communication to foster consensus and empower their employees. Using polls, surveys, feedback, and questionnaires, this leadership style effectively leverages all team members' and stakeholders' diverse ideas, views, and input. This approach is beneficial when managing change and an agile workforce, resulting in optimal outcomes.

Coaching tip: To conduct effective meetings, establish clear rules and boundaries. It's a good idea to document these guidelines in a readily accessible location, such as the company documents section on Breathe. Additionally, we will notify you when your team has reviewed and understood them.

PACESETTING LEADERSHIP STYLE | THE HUSTLER

This type of leadership expects tasks to be completed quickly and efficiently. Therefore, they follow the motto "Do as I do and do it now." This style works well for skilled and driven teams who have tight deadlines. However, there may be better approaches for everyday situations or less-stressful environments.

Although admirable, the drive to succeed and the strong initiative with this leadership style should be approached cautiously. Leaders of this type may unintentionally intimidate and pressure employees due to their intense passion and discipline. Therefore, it's important to empathize and avoid micromanaging employees when considering their workloads.

COACHING LEADERSHIP STYLE | THE MENTOR

The coaching style of leadership prioritizes the growth and development of others, emphasizing a long-term approach. It can be likened to an Italian mother who values the amount of spaghetti eaten as a measure of worth. This leadership style encourages individuals to take each step as progress and emphasizes a strong sense of self. It is characterized by phrases such as "Try this" and "Go on, try some more."

This is how to bring out the best in people: adjust and push the bar for consistent growth while empowering mentees to learn the skills to drive the business forward. Good coaches understand their team and acknowledge that they are always learning, just like their team members.

CHOOSING A LEADERSHIP STYLE

Determining which leadership style suits you best is crucial to successful leadership. Creating a unique style that can adapt to different situations can improve your leadership effectiveness.

1. It's essential to have an understanding of oneself.

To begin, become more aware of your primary leadership approach. Then, to gain insight into the strengths of your leadership style, consider consulting trustworthy colleagues or taking a leadership style assessment.

2. Understand the different styles.

To enhance your leadership skills, it's essential to understand which styles work best in different situations. So what skills do you need to develop to improve?

3. Practice makes a leader.

It's essential to be authentic when using any leadership approach. Switching from a dominant style to another may be difficult initially, but it can become natural with practice. Avoid using a new style as a quick fix. People can easily spot insincerity, so staying true to yourself is best. Authenticity is key.

4. Develop your leadership agility.

Leadership styles from the past are still essential in modern workplaces, but they may need to be adapted to fit the definition of leadership in the 21st century. With a diverse workforce and changing demographics, businesses face many challenges that require a new type of leader who can combine different leadership styles.

In today's workforce, an agile leadership style may be the most effective way to lead and manage talent.

(PCH Coaching Point) DELEGATE

As a principal, I am confident in my leadership approach of delegating duties while still taking full responsibility for the school's overall performance. Of course, it is crucial to fully understand how everything works, but delegating responsibility is a clear indication of effective leadership. To accomplish this, I suggest the following strategies:

1. Work together with your assistant or school secretary to categorize tasks as "mine," "yours," or "ours." Then, let them handle those tasks and inform you of any updates.

2. Encourage teachers to handle discipline issues instead of immediately sending students to the office.

3. Urge parents to speak with assistant principals or teachers about classroom issues before coming to your office. However, I will use my discretion and handle complaints that require immediate attention.

4. Delegate responsibilities to secretaries, school personnel, and parent organizations, allowing them to independently manage their areas of expertise.

YOUR THOUGHTS: ______________________________

____

____

____

____

____

____

____

PRINCIPLE V.

Remember and reflect on your WHY; never forget the reason you CHOOSE to LEAD.

Since becoming an educator, I realized you must always be intentional and have a purpose. I always encourage everyone I contact in the educational setting to establish their "WHY." My why has always been to improve the quality of life for other people! My "WHY" has never been about me as a person or educator; my purpose has been to improve others. Working in education without fully understanding your purpose or having a why is like going to the airport to catch a flight to your destination and arriving without your identification. YOU ARE NOT GOING ANYWHERE! In this case, in your school, when a leader does not have a "Why," their students will ultimately be limited, and their possible destinations will be limited. Your why as a principal should be one of your focal starting points. They are starting with the why is integral to a successful school leader career, and starting with your why is where I would direct all teachers as they begin their careers. And it's where I could run faculty and staff at any stage of their job if it's fallen out of focus.

As an educator, I've learned that purpose and intentionality are crucial. That's why I always encourage those I work with to establish their "WHY" in the educational setting. My goal has always been to improve the quality of life for others and not myself as an individual or educator. Helping others become better is what drives me. However, you work in Education without clearly understanding your purpose or the reason behind your actions. In that case, it is similar to going to the airport without identification to catch a flight. You will need help to get anywhere.

Similarly, if a school leader does not have a clear purpose, their students will be limited in their potential destinations. As a principal, they know your why - your drive and motivation - is essential from the beginning. Starting with this understanding is crucial for success as a school leader. One effective way to improve writing is to provide specific examples or stories that illustrate the importance of having a clear purpose in Education. This approach will help readers better understand the author's perspective and connect with the message personally.

Additionally, emphasizing the advantages of having a clear "why" for educators and students can be an effective strategy. For instance, the author could discuss how a strong sense of purpose can boost classroom motivation, engagement, and achievement.

Furthermore, providing practical strategies or tools that educators can utilize to develop and clarify their "why" is imperative. This could include exercises or prompts that help teachers reflect on their values, goals, and strengths and resources that offer guidance and support for this process.

LET'S GO BACK TO THE BASICS

The principal is responsible for leading the school community, which includes students, teachers, staff, parents, and community partners. They act as a link between the school and the district leadership. School principals oversee the management of all student, teacher, and staff activities.

Many school principals are former classroom teachers who have chosen to advance their careers by taking up this leadership role. Individuals who start as classroom teachers may go to positions such as curriculum specialists, assistant/vice principals, or even school principals. The role of a school principal is crucial, as they play a central part in driving progress within the institution. The specific duties of a principal may vary based on factors like the school's location, student population, and funding resources from the government. Nonetheless, their primary responsibilities can be classified under the following titles:

- Leader: It is imperative that school principals lead the school, establish academic objectives, and supervise the curriculum's progress. Moreover, they must evaluate the teachers and staff members within the campus.
- Administrator: School principals bear the immense responsibility of managing school budgets, ensuring compliance with district, state, and federal policies and regulations, and overseeing the safety and security of the school. They are also accountable for efficiently managing the overall operations of the school.
- Advocate: School principals are strong advocates for their students. They work with teachers confidently to make well-informed decisions that prioritize the needs of their students. Furthermore, they work alongside parents to create plans that promote student success. In addition, principals effectively manage the relationships between students and staff.
- Representative: Principals play a crucial role in representing and advocating for their schools within the district. They tirelessly work towards securing essential resources for both students and teachers while promoting the school's achievements. Moreover, they actively engage with the community during school board meetings and act as the school's public face, projecting a positive image.

Where Does a School Principal Work?

Principals can be found in all types of schools, whether public or private, charter or magnet. It's worth noting that some school leaders may go by a different title, such as lead teacher or head of school. However, their responsibilities in managing the school remain the same.

Various levels of schools cater to different age groups and education needs. These include preschools, elementary schools, middle schools, and high schools. Each level provides a unique learning experience geared towards the development and growth of students.

The duties of a principal can differ from school to school based on several factors, including the school's location, population size, community demographics, budget, and teacher population. For example, in certain schools, principals may work mainly from their office, assisted by an administrative assistant and various vice or assistant principals. However, principals may teach classes or manage clubs or special projects in other schools.

What Do Principals Do?

As a school principal, one has to handle many responsibilities that require a high level of oversight. These include evaluating teachers, keeping track of student performance, managing finances, and engaging with the community. While these tasks can seem daunting, a skilled principal can effectively prioritize and delegate tasks and is ultimately accountable as the leader of their school in various critical areas.

Academic Leadership

As the overseer of academics within a school, the principal has a vital role in ensuring its success. They are responsible for several duties, including evaluating teachers, mentoring them, and conducting classroom observations to assess teachers and students. Moreover, the principal makes decisions relating to curriculum, such as selecting textbooks and implementing new instructional programs or techniques.

In addition, school principals organize events for students, such as inviting guest speakers, arranging assemblies and pep rallies, and attending and leading evening programs, such as science fairs and sports events. They also ensure that teachers receive professional development, training, and conference attendance opportunities to enhance their skills and knowledge.

To foster academic achievement, school principals establish connections with the community and arrange tutoring programs, apprenticeships, and service-learning opportunities for students. With these responsibilities, the school principal plays a crucial part in the education system, ensuring students receive the best education possible.

Strategic Planning

The role of the school principal is vital in leading and approving all strategic planning activities, including creating the academic calendar and introducing new programs and resources. They are responsible for hiring teachers and managing human resources processes, ensuring the school thrives. In addition, the principal oversees student recruitment, admission, and retention, guaranteeing that the school reports accurate numbers and data regarding yearly growth. To comply with district, state, and federal laws, the principal remains up-to-date on all regulations that may impact the school. Moreover, they oversee all aspects of running the school building and its programs, including supervising cafeteria managers, coordinating maintenance technicians, and providing monitors for student supervision during lunch and recess. The principal is also responsible for engaging parents and the community through volunteer programs, making them crucial to the school's success.

Building Community

Outside support is crucial for schools to function. The school principal plays an essential role in engaging with stakeholders, attending PTA/PTO and school board meetings, and addressing critical concerns of the school community. This active involvement helps to ensure the success of the school.

They must communicate with parents regularly about how to best support student success and be transparent about what is happening at school. Principals must establish connections with other school leaders to achieve successful district outcomes. Many schools collaborate with educational companies to obtain resources or implement technology. The principal plays a crucial role in bridging the gap between these companies and the school's staff and students.

Supporting All Students

School principals need to get to know their students to create programs that meet the needs of all learners, including those who require special services and advanced academic opportunities for English language learners. Principals should be prepared to be involved in their student's lives, mainly if they come from unstable family situations or homes without much parental involvement. Principals are responsible for ensuring that every student has an equal opportunity to access a safe and conducive learning environment that enables them to excel academically.

Managing Finances Responsibly.

Managing the school's finances is a crucial responsibility of the school principal. They must thoroughly understand the expenses and efficiently secure additional funding for any needs beyond the approved budget. In addition, payroll and benefits costs are essential considerations for private and independent schools, and principals must ensure that their teachers and staff receive fair compensation. Hence, they must proactively identify areas in the budget where they can make necessary cuts.

Effective School Principals: Key Traits to Look For

To excel in the various responsibilities of their job, school principals need to possess a strong commitment and specific qualities essential for a successful career in school leadership. Moreover, principals must exhibit the following traits to lead a school effectively.

Leadership

Effective school principals play a crucial role in leading their schools to success. They achieve this by actively engaging with students, parents, teachers, and staff and organizing and participating in school events. Additionally, they must make firm decisions that align with the school's objectives.

Communication

Influential leaders must possess excellent communication skills. School principals, for example, should be able to express their thoughts about the school and listen attentively to all parties involved. Despite their numerous responsibilities, they must be fully engaged and attentive during conversations.

Innovation

To be a successful school leader, one must possess excellent problem-solving skills. School principals must use their creativity to identify and solve recurring issues. The role of a school leader demands a great deal of problem-solving, and principals must be able to apply innovative thinking in finding solutions to long-standing problems.

Credibility

School principals are entrusted with confidential personal information about students, parents, teachers, and staff, and they must be able to maintain confidentiality when necessary. Additionally, school principals should be approachable and available to address concerns raised by students and teachers, creating a welcoming and supportive environment.

Fairness

As school leaders, principals should prioritize fairness and establish policies that support and empower students and teachers. This involves implementing disciplinary measures that are just and consistently applied.

Enthusiasm

As a school principal, empowering others by motivating them to succeed is essential. This can be achieved by acknowledging and celebrating student achievements and recognizing teachers' hard work in the classroom. By doing so, the principal can share their enthusiasm and proudly share the school's accomplishments with others interested.

Motivational

A successful leader fosters the growth of other leaders. Therefore, a principal should dedicate time to mentor and guide teachers in developing their leadership skills. Additionally, they should establish a clear vision for the school and facilitate collaboration between students and teachers to achieve shared objectives.

Flexible

As a school principal, it's essential to be flexible and adaptable. Keeping track of the needs of students and staff is crucial, and being prepared to make changes to support them is necessary. Furthermore, staying up-to-date with educational research and experimenting with new techniques to solve old problems is vital to being an effective school principal.

REASONS FOR BECOMING A SCHOOL PRINCIPAL

Becoming a school principal can be a desirable career choice for various reasons. While some individuals enter the teaching profession to become a principal, others may discover that the role would fit them well. Consider the following common reasons why individuals choose to pursue a career as a school principal:

Being a school principal is an incredibly fulfilling career, as most principals report high levels of job satisfaction. Transitioning from a teaching role to a principal position allows for a broader impact on students and the opportunity to develop various skills related to Education and finances. As a school leader, you can set goals and guide the community toward achieving them. Furthermore, with a median annual wage of $90,000 for elementary, middle, and high school principals in May 2022, this career offers a highly competitive salary. As a principal, you can positively influence the school culture and significantly impact academic achievement, college acceptance, extracurricular activities, sports participation, bullying reduction, and school safety. Leading with empathy is critical to making a profound difference in the school's community.

HOW TO BECOME A PRINCIPAL OF A SCHOOL

Becoming a principal does not have a one-size-fits-all approach. The necessary steps vary depending on your current position, whether you're a teacher or a high school student. Nonetheless, you can use the information below as a general guide to help plan your next steps.

- *Obtain a Bachelor's and Master's degree in Education*

If you're currently in high school, it's wise to start planning for your bachelor's degree. In most cases, school principals begin their careers as teachers and then progress to become education administrators. While becoming a principal without prior teaching experience is possible, this is relatively rare. If you're passionate about a particular subject, search for a teaching program that offers initial teaching licensure. It's also advisable to earn a master's degree in educational administration, as many school principals have this qualification. Without a master's degree, there may be fewer opportunities to become a principal.

- *Teaching Experience*

It is recommended to gain several years of teaching experience. While it is possible to specialize in one grade level, teaching different grade levels to gain invaluable experience working with students of various ages is beneficial. This will also help you better understand the needs of teachers at different grade levels.

- *Certification*

In most public schools, principals must have a school administrator credential or license in addition to their teaching license. Private schools may require different certification processes. Many future principals can combine their master's degrees and principal licensure into the same program.

- *Educational Leadership Experience*

Becoming a school principal typically requires having prior school leadership experience. This means that many principals begin their careers as vice or assistant principals. However, there are other ways to gain experience, such as leading a department or serving as a school board representative. Additionally, as a teacher, there are opportunities to explore leadership roles. For example, you can demonstrate your leadership potential by becoming a grade or department chair or working with teachers from different grades to ensure vertical curriculum alignment.

Still, another way to gain school leadership experience is to look for entry-level principal jobs. For example, consider serving as principal at a large school, with an extended reach into the community, or at a small school, where you may work one-on-one with students.

Networking is essential for teachers aspiring to become principals. To achieve this, they should discuss their goals with their current principals and start building connections with leaders in nearby schools. It is also recommended to shadow a principal to understand the job responsibilities better.

(PCH Coaching Point) **STAY A WHILE**

Even after their formal leadership tenures have ended, the "ghosts of the school" rule. They are invisible to the eye and can be found behind your desk. Yet, these are the long line of leaders who have come before you and whose legacies remain.

As a school leader, your responsibility is to create a learning environment that caters to the needs of your students and fosters a community of educators who are committed to this goal. This process takes a significant amount of time. It's crucial to understand that this time frame extends beyond using your current position to advance to a higher-paying job or move up to the central office. Doing this would undermine the profession, your teachers, and your students. Therefore, it's essential to prioritize the growth and development of your school and its community.

Creating a quality school takes time and effort. It is an ongoing process that requires dedication and commitment. However, by investing in this journey, you can profoundly impact the lives of numerous individuals. Your commitment to honesty, care, and a love of learning will be remembered and make a significant difference.

YOUR THOUGHTS:

PRINCIPLE VI.

As often as possible, please show your APPRECIATION

Your team will always work harder when you add value to them, not subtract it. So take this time to ***PRAISE*** your team, no matter what the scoreboard says; celebrate the small gains just as much as you make the significant improvements.

Regularly showing appreciation to your team is crucial to motivate them and increase their value. Don't just focus on significant achievements; celebrate small ones too. Principals should hold celebrations to thank their employees for their hard work and effort throughout the year, strengthening the bond between employers and employees. This helps leaders remember the importance of showing their employees they are valued, regardless of the scoreboard.

We, as school leaders, recognize the challenges of working in a school, but we also know that it is one of the most critical roles in American society. Your dedication, care, and expertise do not go unnoticed by us. So even though you may not receive recognition regularly, we want you to know that your impact on the lives you touch is highly valued and life-affirming.

Appreciating every individual in education who positively impacts our youth's lives is imperative. Teacher Appreciation Week may be celebrated in May in the U.S. Still, the contributions of your faculty, staff, students, and stakeholders are crucial in laying the foundation for the future of this nation. Their efforts should be noticed. As a school leader and community leader, I always found that energy and took the initiative to show everyone in my school community appreciation. If you want your team to work harder:

1. Show them your appreciation.
2. Praise them often to add value to your team, even if they don't win.
3. Remember to celebrate small achievements as much as the big ones.

Here are 15 ways to show your team how much you appreciate their effort.

1. Motivate your children or pupils to unleash their creativity by drawing or taking a photo and adding it to a note they compose themselves. Encourage them to begin with phrases such as "You taught me this year..." or "I appreciate you for..." Ensure they acknowledge all the key players, including the principal, secretary, custodian, and bus driver.
2. If you want to express gratitude to people making a positive difference in the lives of others, sending a handwritten note is a beautiful way to do so. It doesn't need to be extravagant; simply highlighting a specific attribute that sets them apart is enough. In addition, this gesture is an excellent way to demonstrate that you value and admire their contributions.
3. To show appreciation for their favorite teachers or school personnel, encourage parents and website visitors to share their thoughts on your school website's form. You'll likely receive positive feedback by making it easy for them to express gratitude. Include questions on the condition that encourage people to share their thoughts.
4. Regarding your website content, consider adding a feature allowing alumni to comment. This could be done through a form on either the district or high school websites and would be a valuable tool for displaying feedback.

5. You must take the initiative to call a school staff member and express your appreciation for their unwavering dedication, regardless of the time of day or week. Ensure you provide concrete examples of your gratitude for their hard work.

6. Consider hiring a massage therapist to bring their chair to your school for the day. Encourage your staff to use this opportunity during their prep, lunch break, or before/after school. Chair massages are less disruptive than full body massages and are a great way to show appreciation for your hardworking staff.

7. Consider treating your school community to an "Appreciation" luncheon or breakfast. Arrange for a catered meal and hire some substitutes to take over classes, rotating as needed. This will allow your faculty and staff to enjoy the event without feeling rushed. You can also turn in grade levels to have the opportunity to visit with each staff member personally.

8. Public praise is a highly effective way to show appreciation that is often overlooked. Teachers and other school community members work hard and deserve recognition. Why not share the good deeds of your peers with others in your school? One teacher we spoke to said, "Being praised in front of your colleagues is one of the most fulfilling experiences. As teachers, we spend most of our day behind closed doors and rarely see what our colleagues are doing. If you like what you see, let the rest of the staff know!" We couldn't agree more. Public praise is a cost-effective way to express gratitude and respect to your staff. Take advantage of your school's social media to acknowledge the achievements of your staff, students, and administrators every chance you get. Take advantage of the opportunity to celebrate the hard work of your team!

9. Suppose you want to acknowledge a staff member or celebrate a special event like their retirement, teaching anniversary, or earning a master's degree. In that case, you can buy a book for the school library. Allow the staff member to choose the book they want and include a commemorative bookplate inside.

10. As a gesture of gratitude, offering kolaches or donuts in the morning would be nice. Also, Boudin and cupcakes make for delightful treats if you are in Louisiana.

11. It is highly recommended that a spotlight section be created on your school's website and social media accounts. This section should feature a different staff member every few weeks or each month.

12. Reminding students to express gratitude towards their teachers during daily announcements is essential. To facilitate this, notecards and envelopes can be provided at the front office, allowing students to write personal messages to their teachers. Alternatively, an online form can be created on the school website, allowing students to email their notes directly to the staff members. In the event of snow days causing the loss of school vacations, offering special treats on makeup days is recommended to acknowledge the additional stress caused by losing essential planning days or vacation time.

13. One way to improve the teachers' lounge is by requesting your PTA or PTO to add some fresh paint, pictures, curtains, and new or gently used furniture to make it more cozy and inviting. During Teacher Appreciation Week, you can use social media to show appreciation. Encourage your classes to hold thank you signs, take pictures and post them on Facebook, Twitter, and Instagram. You can also create a Pinterest board and share photos, quotes, and memories that showcase teachers' positive impact on their students. Remember to invite alums to participate in the celebration.

14. During Teacher Appreciation Week, it's essential to showcase your school community's participation in various activities and events to the local media. This promotes your school and recognizes your teachers' hard work and dedication. It's a powerful way to appreciate your staff and make your school stand out in the community. By benefiting your team, you can also improve your school's reputation.

15. It is essential to regularly express gratitude towards school employees, volunteers, teachers, and administrators. Take the opportunity to do so at meetings, in the hallway, or at conferences. Additionally, consider showing your appreciation on your social media account. Be specific about their contributions, and remember to acknowledge birthdays and anniversaries. You can even include a photo of the honored person to make it more personal.

As school leaders, we must always look for ways to build our team up and strengthen them. One of the primary roles of the principal is to create a culture of mutual respect and build up supporters' capacity around them. Consistently showing appreciation and praising everyone within the building can groom any group into a productive team. Principals must learn each identity to understand how to make the acts of appreciation intentional. Expressing gratitude towards faculty, staff, students, and the school community is essential to creating a positive and efficient workplace that contributes to enhanced teaching and student achievements. In addition, it's a critical aspect of delivering exceptional customer service in schools. By implementing positive practices and inspiring others to do the same, you can establish a dependable, supportive, and enjoyable team atmosphere that boosts staff morale. Remember that starting with small steps is no issue; the crucial thing is to take action immediately!

(PCH Coaching Point) PRIORITIZE PLANNING

As a new principal, it's normal to feel overwhelmed by the fast pace of the school day. But with a bit of planning, you can stay on top of everything. First, utilize modern technology to sync your calendar with your staff and ensure everyone is on the same page. Then, work closely with your assistant principals and secretaries to create a plan for the week ahead, meet with staff regularly, and delegate tasks effectively. By taking a coordinated approach, you can confidently lead your school toward success.

YOUR THOUGHTS:

4TH QUARTER

MOTIVATE YOUR TEAM
TO FINISH THE DAY
NO MATTER WHAT HAS OCCURRED.
REGARDLESS OF WHAT
IT LOOKS LIKE,
REMAIN POSITIVE.

4TH QUARTER

Motivate your team to FINISH the day no matter what has occurred. Regardless of what it looks like, remain POSITIVE.

Ultimately we would like to win at everything we do, but we must remember that their no such thing as losses or taking an "L", instead we consider we always win two "L's" lessons learned!

In all aspects of school leadership, we must remember that although management is a significant part of our job, motivation carries even more weight. Just as in sports, the coaches must make sure they have everyone on their team motivated so they can be in a position to win; principals have the same responsibility. Coaches can only do it some, and neither can principals. As a principal, I always wanted everyone on my team to win! Daily I set out to inspire and empower everyone who entered my building and came to work. My expectation was simple, I expected a willingness to be motivated and for everyone to possess a tool of self-motivation as well. Principals must encourage their faculty, staff, and students with passion, focus, discipline, and strong beliefs. And we must find ways to be intentional and consistent in the actions that it takes to get the results that we desire to achieve.

How many times have we, as school leaders, led an extraordinary faculty meeting to motivate the team, and everyone exhibits total "ALL IN" actions and sentiments, only to see the same energy and enthusiasm fade shortly afterward? We must always be mindful that motivation is easy to jumpstart but often hard to sustain. Motivating our staff requires good nutrition and hydration. Therefore, we must repeatedly enhance it. It works just like our bodies work, and if we do not continue to refuel it with the proper nutrients and proteins, it will not perform consistently to our satisfaction. Athletes in all professional sports usually abide by a regime that keeps them motivated to work out and eat right all year; besides financial incentives in their lucrative contracts, longevity and health throughout their career is a typical denominator regarding motivation. Unfortunately, when school leaders need to motivate their staff consistently, it usually yields a lack of systems, leading to a lack of proper preparation, poor performances, potential learning loss, and low morale.

Systems are what makes teams great, not necessarily the people. Nick Saban is a great coach, one of the best. Each year he loses many players to the N.F.L. draft and graduation, coaches who fulfill their dream of being a head coach, and recruits to other Power 5 colleges. Yet, perennially he continues to field some of the best college football teams each year! WHY? HOW? It's because he creates excellent systems. A system is a focused plan in which principals must get involved to implement critical activities and desired results consistently. Objectives are inclusive of methods that can be achieved through incentives. As a principal, not only was I a significant fan of P.B.I.S. (Positive Behavior Interventions and Supports) for students, but I developed an extensive P.B.I.S. plan for my adults on campus to keep them motivated and engaged in the work they do. You must take care of your people, regardless of what the scoreboard says, when trying to win the day, week, month, semester, or school year. During my principalship, I learned that most of my staff responded to three major categories; my challenges, my energy, and my teaching.

Regarding my challenges, I realized earlier in my career that educators love challenges; in fact, it's of the reasons they entered the field of education. When I issued larger areas of responsibility to specific staff members, they usually looked at it as a compliment, a new level of trust, and gifted ownership. To them, it was a sign that I, as the school leader, believed in them and their capabilities, which motivated them to do more! Every week I would start with my team meetings and then meet individually with each person on the team. I would create a challenge for the week that wasn't connected to some recognition or reward but was tied to creating new levels of understanding beyond their initial job description. This activity allowed me to delegate equally and grow my capacity rapidly amongst the team members. However, as a principal, always remember that you can delegate duties, but you cannot delegate responsibilities. EVERYTHING is your RESPONSIBILITY! This system allows you to make more sound decisions quickly and with extraordinary collaborative efforts. Be mindful that as a leader, you must constantly surround yourself with "motivated" people." When you put a person with potential and can be motivated to see the more significant picture/outcome. As the principal for those not inspired around you, it is your responsibility to help them find motivation. If, after your efforts, it still does not work, then you should create a detailed plan to allow them to grow into the team member that you need them to be.

Regarding my energy, As a principal, you must challenge yourself to be the most positive, energetic, empowering person on your campus daily! If you want your team to have the right energy, you must have it so that your faculty, staff, and students can feel it in what you say and, most importantly, what you do. In sports, it is critical that coaches believe in all the principles of coaching and that they follow the game plan in their playbook. Coaches, just like principals, must be passionate about them. Principals must know that a positive attitude and the energy that comes from it can motivate the team to overcome any obstacle or loss.

Consequently, principals must understand that a negative attitude can be cancerous, and just like the disease itself, it can kill your culture and poison your environment. Positive energy and a passion for you can motivate any bad team and lead to overall success. On the other hand, negative energy, along with a lack of love, will motivate the team to fail. Principal walk-throughs are so important, not just because of the data collection involved but also because it allows everyone to see you and what you represent at that particular time. When the principal engages with everyone positively, it creates an atmosphere where everyone wants to get better in every aspect.

Regarding my teaching, As a principal, you must know that you are not only the lead learner on campus but also the lead teacher on campus. I have always told myself I wanted to create more leaders, not followers! One way I accomplished that feat was to teach everyone who wanted to learn everything that I had learned. This concept is simple yet very productive in school leadership. As a principal, the mentality must be created that we must continually grow our team, not just maintain our order of operations. A leadership team can get more accomplished and achieve the results they are looking for when a principal teaches and conveys the knowledge and skill set they have to people who can take it and expand it within their role. This action can lead to an increase in morale, not a decrease, which a principal should always be responsible for. When the principal serves as the lead teacher, they also can control change and monitor the pulse checks of the school. We should make it a habit to acknowledge the current hardships, circumstances, and great things occurring during our teachings. Similar to halftime speeches, In football, coaches tend to give lessons before the game(pregame), during the match (timeouts), at halftime, and after the game (post-game analysis. This is a similar format that principals should follow throughout the day and the school year. In the pregame, principals should be the leader and motivators to prepare everyone for the school year. At midterms(halftime), the principal should always have short messages that help redirect everyone and make adjustments to what the initial game plan was. When making adjustments, the principal should always employ teachable moments to get everyone back on track and ready to resume the chasing of the goals or victory. During timeouts (faculty meetings, P.L.C.s, departmental meetings, etc.), The principal should teach to correct the moment, making changes that can create a decision causing everyone to pivot for the better. Lastly, during the post-game meetings (end-of-year evaluations, projections, planning), the principal's teaching mode should focus on recognizing the good and the bad of the school year and concentrate on what is to come.

It is helpful to get to know them well to maintain a positive attitude and keep your team motivated to finish strong during the school year. As a principal, I imagined a "bubble" over every person on my campus. Inside that imaginary bubble was a story that revealed the unique aspects of each person's personality. Knowing your staff well is crucial to motivate them to reach the finish line. During the first few days of school, take the opportunity to discover what makes your team happy. Find their favorite beverages (hot and cold), songs, snacks, games, colors, T-shirt sizes, and hobbies. This information can be utilized to customize significant events in the upcoming months, such as surprises, awards, and tokens of appreciation.

To help teachers get off to a good start, it is important to provide them with the necessary tools such as whiteboards, extra paper, bookshelves, rugs, and functioning air conditioning. Having everything they need to do their job can make a huge difference. Additionally, since time is a valuable commodity for teachers, finding ways to give them more time can be greatly appreciated. It is recommended to check your temperature before entering the premises. Furthermore, maintaining a positive mood in a school setting is not solely the principal's responsibility. Other team members, such as teachers, assistant principals, and instructional coaches, who possess expertise, experience, wisdom, and likable personalities, already have established connections with the staff and can boost morale. It's essential to build relationships and show empathy towards teachers. They have personal responsibilities outside of work and may need support. Show genuine concern for their family and personal life, and get to know them better. This will help you notice if something seems off and address it before it becomes problematic. Shared activities, like playing games or having a meal together, can also strengthen bonds between principals and staff. Finally, keeping teachers informed about what's happening is important to reduce uncertainty and anxiety.

The school principal has taken on the role of the school's mental health leader in light of the increasing demands placed on students and employees at the school with regard to mental health issues. Due to the inexperience of most building leaders, the role of a building leader in the area of mental health is one of the more challenging ones due to the fact that they have not been trained in mental health as a subject matter. As a leader, it is essential that you understand and develop a self-care strategy well before you find yourself actually in need of it. Primary and secondary trauma can take a number of forms, and it is important to realize that they can occur in different ways. It was not only compassion fatigue that we experienced, but we also experienced a student suicide as part of our trauma experience as well. As a result of the Coronavirus outbreak and the catastrophic events of Hurricanes Laura and Delta in the past few months, principals across the country and in particular my area have experienced a new trauma in the form of a new trauma. Since the opening of the schools for the 2020-21 school year, it had become evident that principals were aware of the plight of students and staff who had suffered a wide range of losses since the start of the new school year. Students and staff both experienced a wide spectrum of losses during their time at the university, from losing a job to losing a loved one. This school year, building principals have been under a great deal of scrutiny for the decisions they have made regarding the safety of students and staff at their schools. It has been reported that the opinions of the community regarding those safeguards range from "not doing enough" to "doing too much". In addition to the added responsibilities that come with the position of principal, a school's burden for these responsibilities can certainly add weight to the school's load that would otherwise not be there. There is no doubt that taking care of oneself is of the utmost importance for leaders this year, and it could not be more true.

Our experiences have taught us that it is imperative that we take care of ourselves on a daily basis if we are to maintain good mental health in the long run. Taking care of ourselves must be prioritized and recognized as a sign of strength, not weakness, and that it is a sign of strength to take care of ourselves. Due to the fact that we have multiple roles to fulfill every day, it is important that we establish boundaries between our personal and professional lives in order to avoid conflict. It is important to note that self-care can be as simple or as significant as one wishes, such as laughing, which can also be considered to be an act of self-care in and of itself. Taking the time to take care of ourselves is a great way to make sure that our staff members prioritize their own well-being while practicing the same self-care that we practice on our own.

It's no secret that there are many of us who consider the principalship to be our calling. I would like to express my sincere gratitude to you for taking the call and answering it in such a timely manner. While our job may be rewarding, it can also be lonely and isolating at times as principals, even though it is a rewarding job. It is strongly recommended that you reach out to the principals in your neighborhood in order to establish a network of professionals with whom you can talk, encourage, and hold each other accountable to take care of yourself so that you can stay healthy. The most important thing for you to remember is that you must take care of yourself before you can take care of others. If you ask me, the one thing I always tell educators is that if you don't have water, then you can't pour from an empty cup.

(PCH Coaching Point) SUPERVISION AND EVALUATION OF PERSONNEL

The evaluation of personnel is a crucial responsibility of a principal, regardless of the state's requirements. It is important to maintain positive and constructive interaction between the principal and staff through frequent and informal evaluations. The superintendent should encourage this interaction. The effective instructional coaching the superintendent and central office team provides is crucial, regardless of the district's evaluation plan. This coaching should occur in the schools, be ongoing, and include frequent classroom walkthroughs with the principal.

YOUR THOUGHTS:

PRINCIPLE VII

Continue REINFORCING EFFORT. Keep everyone positive and active. The results will move you closer to the outcome that you desire. Be effective and efficient in improving the outcomes of student learning, staff development, and overall growth.

The key relationships in the ways school leaders strengthen teacher recruitment, development and retention while continuing to reinforce the effort of their staff members include many factors such as teacher satisfaction, school effectiveness, improvement, capacity, teacher leadership, distributive leadership, organizational learning, and development. Principals can be a major influence on these school-level factors as well as help buffer against the excesses of the mounting and sometimes contradictory external pressures. A skilled and well-supported leadership team in schools can help foster a sense of ownership and purpose in the way that teachers approach their job. Conferring professional autonomy to teachers will enhance the attractiveness of the profession as a career choice and will improve the quality of the classroom teaching practice. Teachers who work together in a meaningful and purposeful ways have been found to be more likely to remain in the profession because they feel valued and supported in their work. Many school experts suggests that while decentralization may have occurred from the system to school level, it has not necessarily occurred within schools. Further, where decentralization has occurred within schools it tended to be about administrative rather than education matters. This situation should be of concern, especially given evidence teachers are attracted to, and stay in, the profession if they feel they belong and believe they are contributing to the success of their school and students.

One of the most consistent findings from studies of effective school leadership is that authority to lead need not be located in the person of the leader but can be dispersed within the school between and among people. There is a growing understanding that leadership is embedded in various organizational contexts within school communities, not centrally vested in a person or an office. The real challenge facing most schools is no longer how to improve but, more importantly, how to sustain improvement. Sustainability will depend upon the school's internal capacity to maintain and support developmental work and sustaining improvement requires the leadership capability of the many rather than the few. Principals must be effective and efficient in improving the outcomes of student learning, staff development, and overall growth evermore with the job description and role of a principal becoming too demanding, stressful, lonely, lacking support, and only for select groups in the world. in keeping with working smarter and not harder, it's paramount that everything a school leader does should have a focus on improving the instruction in the school. I suggest the following steps for principals:

- *Define a clear vision and mission for the school.*
- *Establish a transparent administrative structure.*
- *Ensure instructional consistency by using a walk-through tool like BULLSEYE to observe classroom activities.*
- *Encourage a coaching culture to set an example for the administrative team.*

It's essential to stay informed about necessary school data such as attendance records for teachers and students, behavioral patterns, end-of-course assessments, graduation rates, course failures, and individual growth plans for students. In addition, principals, assistant principals, instructional coaches, and deans must create an effective professional development plan for all staff members, including support personnel. As an evaluator, this is a critical daily duty that principals undertake. Although it can be challenging, it is possible to do it well. To improve student performance, it is imperative to assess the school's social, emotional, and instructional aspects and ensure that all resources are aligned. To achieve this, you can use the questions above as a template for root-cause analysis and assess the current state of your school.

It's important to remember that our instructional day and work week have limited time. That's why ensuring everyone stays positive and active with intentionality is crucial. Doing so will help us achieve our desired outcome and improve student learning, staff development, and overall growth. Although we can't be everywhere, our presence and the systems we create can still be felt throughout our buildings.

To enhance the instructional focus of your building and strengthen your staff and systems on campus, consider asking yourself these reflective questions:

- *Can you provide information on our school's educational goals and objectives? Additionally, what is the current atmosphere and attitude within our school community? Should there be any changes in focus, how do you plan to address them?*
- *Does our school prioritize providing our students with a high-quality education, or do we place more emphasis on extracurricular activities and social media presence?*
- *How do we recognize and celebrate the achievements of our students and educators?*
- *According to the principal, all assistant principals and instructional coaches know their responsibilities and expectations regarding good instruction.*
- *Do we use a walk-through and rubric tool to support instructional efforts?*
- *Have we received training in a coaching model to ensure we meet expectations?*
- *Is there a system to monitor student performance regarding course completion and state assessments?*
- *Is there a belief that quality instruction leads to improved student outcomes?*

- *Do we currently have a professional development program and a way to assess its impact?*

School leadership plays an essential role in establishing an effective learning environment. To enhance student outcomes, staff development, and overall growth, it's crucial to identify your unique strengths. While every leader might not possess all these strengths, understanding your values, stability, and weaknesses can help you leverage your attributes and find teammates with complementary qualities. Share your motivations with your team to get them invested in your goals. Here are some examples to consider.

DEEP THINKING IS THE KEY TO SUCCESS

People who think deeply may only sometimes express their thoughts as much as others. However, they are still processing, reflecting, and making meaningful connections. Instead, they take their time and are skilled at considering the effects on individuals and systems before making decisions. If you are one of these deep thinkers, make it known that you require time to process information and decide. It is also important to revisit any unresolved topics. Additionally, sharing your thoughts with others can be beneficial as it allows for a metacognitive process that can offer insights for those who tend to speak first and think later.

EMOTIONAL CONNECTIONS

If you can gauge the emotions in a room and adapt accordingly, you possess a valuable strength. Additionally, if you have ever delivered a speech that deeply moved your audience, you likely have a talent for connecting with people on an emotional level. This strength can unite your school community towards a common goal while showing understanding and compassion towards others. However, it is important to avoid becoming overwhelmed by taking on the emotions of others too profoundly or by internalizing criticisms directed at your position or institution rather than at you as an individual.

THE IMPORTANCE OF OPEN COLLABORATION

Collaborative leaders are those who seek the input and ideas of others when faced with a problem to solve. They recognize that collective wisdom is more powerful than their own and celebrate the talents of those around them. While they may be humble, they are not afraid to showcase the abilities of their team, inspiring and building shared efficacy. Collaborators also understand the importance of accepting praise and credit when due, even when it means promoting their achievements.

AN EFFECTIVE APPROACH TO ANALYZING

In addition to being proficient in data analysis, principals who possess strong analytical skills need data in order to make sense of all that they are responsible for managing. This ability to analyze programs, performance, and actions on the basis of concrete measures is undervalued in public education, and it is a critically important skill. Besides being able to see the patterns and outcomes, if you can question, interpret, and articulate those patterns and outcomes to others, the analytical skills you possess will be of great use to you. In your sphere, many of us are much less comfortable with data, so you will need to explain to us the story of what the data represents in order to get us on board with digging deeper into it.

A CREATIVE APPROACH TO ENVISIONING

In uncertain spaces-where innovation is required-some, principals are comfortable with the "big picture," while others are terrified of it. There is no doubt that having a vision for your school, and more importantly, bringing in stakeholders to make that vision a shared vision, is one of the most critical attributes for principals. You are fortunate if this comes naturally to you; however, you should keep in mind that many people are skeptical about "vision people," wondering if they will follow through when it comes down to the nitty-gritty details of what they have planned. To build trust and shared ownership within your administrative team and on your campus, you need to combine creativity and vision with boots-on-the-ground implementation so that you can create a culture of trust and shared ownership.

(PCH Coaching Point) POLITICAL AWARENESS AND SUPPORT

As a new principal, the superintendent can be a valuable resource in understanding the community's political landscape. In addition, they can provide insights into how various power brokers influence the school and offer advice on gaining community support.

To ensure a prosperous and harmonious work environment, the principal must establish firm boundaries and cultivate positive relationships with the various groups with political influence, including the PTO/PTA, the local collective bargaining union, and the informal faculty leaders at each school.

Once the district has found the ideal candidate for the principal position, the superintendent and central administrators must provide the necessary support for their success. Although the job description may be extensive, being a principal is commendable. It is crucial to ensure that the system in place supports the principal and regularly recognizes and appreciates their commitment, effort, and contribution to the school district.

YOUR THOUGHTS:

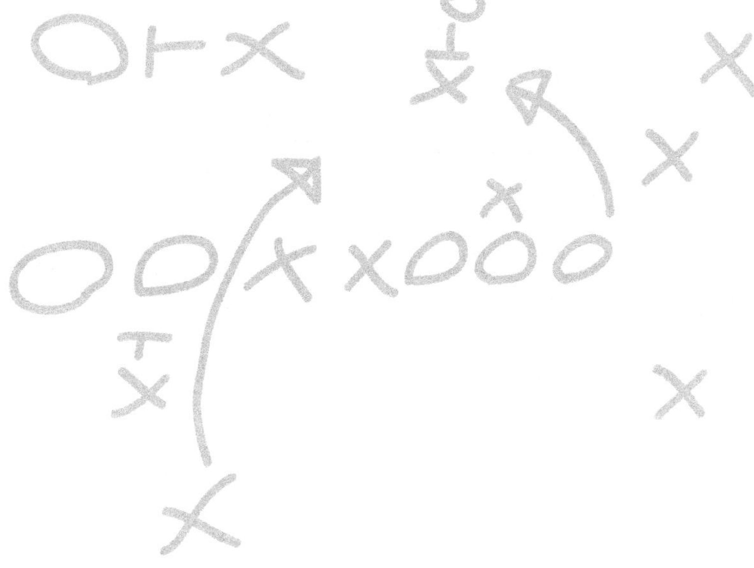

POST-GAME ANALYSIS

IT'S THE PRINCIPALS' JOB TO **REVIEW** THE PERFORMANCE OF THE TEAM; GATHER THEIR OPINIONS, WEIGH THE PROS AND CONS, THEN APPLY THEM ACCORDINGLY. REMEMBER THE GAME HAS JUST BEGUN!

POST-GAME ANALYSIS

It's the principals' job to REVIEW the performance of the team; gather their opinions, weigh the pros and cons, then apply them accordingly. Remember the game has just begun!

If you've been supporting and evaluating teachers all year, keep that work from fading out as summer approaches. Instead, make sure you and your teachers get the most out of the year by having a formal close-out conversation. You can initiate this meaningful conversation as a teacher rather than an instructional leader. Five steps can help guide you through this critical exchange of information.

Focus on Teacher Strengths

Regardless of a teacher's experience level, acknowledging their strengths is the most effective way to set a positive tone for the upcoming school year. Teaching can be stressful, especially for new ones, so focusing on the positives at the end of the year can help boost their confidence and make them feel empowered for the next year instead of questioning their ability to continue.

Identify Focus Areas for Next Year

The summer offers a great time for professional development and personal reflection, but this will only happen if teachers feel motivated and excited to do it. So even if you know where you want teachers to focus on improving, now is the time to give them complete ownership over their development so that it's meaningful for them and they're inspired to do it.

Create a Summer/Fall Action Plan

Since teachers are ready to plunge into their hard-earned summer vacation, what this action plan looks like will depend on the teacher. They should lead the ideas for these next steps based on whatever meaningful focus areas you have identified together. For example, some teachers might have many ideas for the conferences, planning, and prep they want to do over the summer. For others, their summer commitment might be minimal, and the conversation will be more about what they'll do when they return in the fall. Either way, you're giving them a concrete plan to focus on as they think about next school year.

Clear the Path

This phrase comes from the book Switch by Chip and Dan Heath. Clearing the path is about removing as many barriers as possible so that an action or change is most likely to happen. In these final conversations with teachers, clearing the path is about thinking through the details of the teachers' next steps and removing barriers so that they can visualize these steps happening and articulate how they'll happen. For example, if a teacher is interested in writing three unit plans over the summer, talk through their summer plans to help identify which weeks would be available for writing them and what resources they would need. Then, depending on the teacher's level of enthusiasm, you can calendar out when everything will happen. With this clear path to success, it's easier for the summer weeks to fly by; suddenly, it's the first day back at school, and the teacher still needs to accomplish the summer plans they intended to.

Get Some Feedback

Find out from the teachers you support what they appreciated about your support, what they wanted more of, and what they'd want to change. This conversation could happen in person, but it could also be through an anonymous survey if you'd get more honest feedback. Again, this is mutually beneficial because it helps them identify what they need from a coach or evaluator, enabling you to gain insight into how to support your teachers better next year.

No matter what stresses and trials you and your teachers may have faced this year, closing the year strong with positive, actionable takeaways will ensure that teachers walk away feeling empowered, inspired, and ready to return even stronger next year!

CHALK TALK

CHALK TALK

It will be a great day, when we all understand that one of the best test of our faith is when we can do things for others who may never be able to do things for us in return. Often times those people are the children of today! We as adults have to ensure that we are not doing things in favor of wanting something in return. If we love children and believe they are our future; then we must act in a way that we continue pay our interest in them forward, simply in hopes of moving them FORWARD, ONWARD, and UPWARD in all phases of life. Reach one and teach one today. May the blessings be with everyone along this jOURney.

When times get tough, remember it's just a plot in your story, but it's not the way your story has to end. Be positive and activate your faith. Greater faith leads to greater favor. This year we all are moving forward, onward, and upward; write your chapters the way you believe that should be written. Believe all things are possible, and let your faith be greater than your fear.

Every season ends with a championship. Are you preparing to get to the big game in your season or are you not preparing at all? Proper Preparation Prevents Poor Performances. Remember faith without work is dead, believe that the impossible is possible! This is your season to move forward, onward, and upward.

UNIQUELY YOU

Know that you were created with a pUrpose and with intentions to make an impact on the world around you! The plans were for good and not disaster with potential outcomes for a future and for hope. Let's embrace the fact that our design was intentional. There is no problem too big to be solved, all we have to do is BELIEVE.

THE BLINDSPOT

As drivers, we are aware that when driving our vehicle, one of the most dangerous areas around our vehicle is referred to as the "BLINDSPOT." This is the area that you cannot see using your mirrors. The only way to check your BLINDSPOT is to turn your head and check. In the journey of moving forward, onward, and upward; we must always be cognizant of our blindspots. Often times that area contains, distractions, haters, naysayers, dream killers, and pitfalls. Remember to stay focused on moving ahead, but check blindspots from time to time just so you can monitor how far you are moving in the the right direction.

Past experiences have taught me to stay away from negative people. They usually have a problem for every solution. However, the knowledge I have gained from those experiences is teaching me to realize that they were lessons and blessings in the process. Trusting this jOURney...

One of my main goals going forward is to help people get tougher. We must develop a growth mindset of an overcomer, realizing that we all will go through cycles of "hard or tough" times. However, if we continuously condition ourselves to be stronger for not only ourselves but others too, eventually things will subside. Let's continue to move forward, onward, and upward regardless of the obstacle that's in front of us.

To understand sometimes you have to take yourself out the frame to see the bigger picture, it's all about helping everyone else move forward, onward, and upward.

When sitting in the exit row on a plane, the flight attendant will usually pose two questions: (1) In the event of an emergency, are you willing and able to assist everyone in need? (2) Do you understand that we are asking you to make sure you help everyone before assisting yourself?

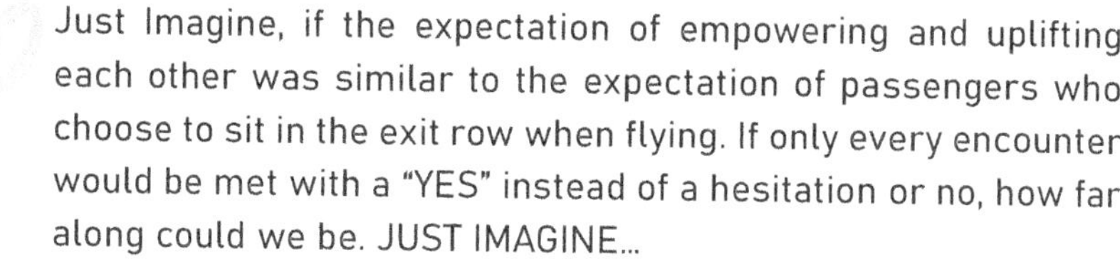

Just Imagine, if the expectation of empowering and uplifting each other was similar to the expectation of passengers who choose to sit in the exit row when flying. If only every encounter would be met with a "YES" instead of a hesitation or no, how far along could we be. JUST IMAGINE...

Stay focused. When people write ✍ you off, you don't have to write ✍ back! Just keep intentionally moving forward, onward, and upward, into the next chapter and watch how the narrative changes in your favor. You are an author, and you reserve the right to write ✍ your own story. People's opinion of you is none of your business!

PUBLIC SERVICE ANNOUNCEMENT

Always remember that there will always be a plot (positive/negative) against you and your movement. At times, it may feel like you are losing the fight and maybe even the war. Stay positive keep navigating forward, onward, and upward.

Remember this battle is not yours.

Perspective is everything

When the mentality is crafted with a foundation of truly moving forward, onward, and upward in all walks of life. One must remember that along this jOURney, you must stay cool, calm, and collected. The pathway chosen has seen few venture in the direction, but many sit back and watch the movement as if it's an adventure.

STAY FOCUSED! It's your lane, not everyone else's. Let's make it a great day, the choice is yours!

If you feel you haven't been productive or progressing lately, it's okay it is part of the process which ultimately leads to the outcomes that your heart desires. Dust yourself off and keep moving forward, onward, and upward. We are one moment or one encounter away from changing the trajectory of our life and others, stay the course. Remember the blessings are along the jOURney as well as at the end.

Your mindset and your thoughts will take you places and open doors of opportunity that you could never imagine. The key ingredients are action and faith, for without them you will only experience doubt and limitations. There will never be a perfect time to move forward, onward, and upward; if you continue to allow others to cast doubt on your ultimate goals.

We must always be mindful of "THE CROWD," along with the positives and negatives of having one! With all the negativity, hatred, and self-destruction that's occurring in this world daily, one must stop and ask "Would the effects be the same if there was no crowd?" When intentionality truly exist and purposeful energy for change co-exist, we will start to see the transformation of the way society is and the way we view society. (Perspective)

Take some time and ignore the crowd (respectfully), be your authentic self regardless of whether the crowd is roaring in celebration of you or screaming in hatred of you. Continuously, remember your "Why" and keep moving forward, onward, and upward. Let's make it a great day, the choice is yours.

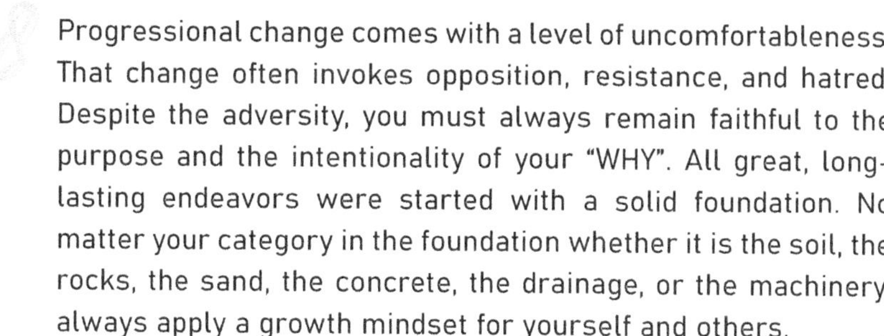

18 Progressional change comes with a level of uncomfortableness. That change often invokes opposition, resistance, and hatred. Despite the adversity, you must always remain faithful to the purpose and the intentionality of your "WHY". All great, long-lasting endeavors were started with a solid foundation. No matter your category in the foundation whether it is the soil, the rocks, the sand, the concrete, the drainage, or the machinery; always apply a growth mindset for yourself and others.

19 Keep moving at your pace and persisting in your "WHY," while propelling others forward, onward, and upward.

20 Always guard your brand and your identity at all cost! Be mindful that there will be some who will stand and clap for you one minute, then sit and hate you the next minute!

21 Always be confident in the person you are becoming and never forget your WHY! Perspective is everything, always look at the glass half full versus half empty!

22 Let's make it a great day, the choice is yours! May blessings continue along this jOURney.

23 In order for Us to change oUr circUmstances in oUr cUltURe, we have to first hold oUrselves accoUntable for oUr actions. This JoUrney starts with the person who we see when we look in the mirror.

OURSELVES

You are the number #1 determinant factor in the results you want to have within the outcomes you desire. Believe that everything YOU hope for is possible. May the blessings be with Us along yOUR jOURney!

All storms were not created equally! Every storm isn't sent to break, destroy, or disrupt your life. Some of the storms have a purpose; some storms are driven to prepare you for what God truly has in store for you. Embrace what you have to overcome, he never said it would be easy, but it will be worth it! Get prepared for this season, your winning season is already scheduled!

Don't just survive the storm, but thrive instead!

As a school community, we must stop making errors that are causing the results that we are seeing each and everyday in our youth. We have begun to normalize "unforced errors" as if we are trying to be intentional in taking a pathway to destruction.

In my interpretation, "unforced errors" means that no one forced you to make the mistake; it was self-created, self-inflicted, and ultimately leads to self-destruction.

We must understand that some of the mistakes that we as adults are making daily are allowing our youth to normalize the mistakes they see us making. How can we honestly expect our kids to "WIN" or act better when they are falling in love with the "unforced errors" that they see us as adults making everyday.

If we truly want to move forward, onward, and upward; we must find solutions and stop making more excuses! Generational curses are real, and making more "unforced errors" is not an indicator or sign of change.

✓ when we fight = they fight

✓ when we quit = they quit

✓ when we negative = they negative

✓ when we are violent = they are violent

✓ when we let the enemy/opposition enter = they welcome the enemy/opposition

---

When we get to the point we realize that we can all be great together, it will be something special to witness.

We must develop the mentality to develop greatness WITH everyone, not be greater than everyone! It's a mindset!

"I like being great with you, I don't need to be greater than you"

It's almost impossible for everything to be good or for everything to be bad. For every positive action there will be an equal yet opposite reaction. Moral of the story: Control the narrative! Write your own story and share it with the world! Never give someone else the power to write, change, or tell YOUR story!

WE are struggling as a society, as a community, and as a culture because WE are not being authentic. Some of us have created a false disconnect between what's real and what's fake. The art of living and breathing the message that you convey to others daily in a consistent manner is when it's genuine. There should be no disconnect between your personal values and your professional image, alignment is key. WE must also remember that as a village; its always easier to tear down, but it's always worth it to build up, the children are always watching...

No one is going to believe in your dreams or goals like you do. Stop expecting everyone to support your vision or your calling, it wasn't a conference call, to begin with. Stay humble, and keep serving while moving forward, onward, and upward.

Admire the naysayers, they too are in position for you to make them out of a believer. No matter what opposition, adversity, or level of uncertainty comes your way; remember your why, smile and keep moving forward, onward and upward!

Consistent action with consistent commitment can change the results of any experience. When moving forward, onward, and upward, you must have a never quit mindset, delays are to be expected but denial is to never be accepted.

ASSIGNMENT FOR TODAY...

Focus on your lane! Don't pay so much attention to what's going on in your rearview and side view mirrors (negative people)! Focus on where you are going and stop giving attention to the detours planted by other people (distractions). People's opinion of you should not define you and actually; it's none of your business. It's theirs! Let the pathway you take today create the destination you want to be at on tomorrow! Focus on staying in your lane while sitting in the driver's seat, and watch how you cruise forward, onward, and upward!

The art of raising children is not an instant challenge, a trend, or temporary effort from a social media post. We must strategically rebuild the village to be consistent and robust enough to raise the whole child. At some point, the action of "it takes a village to raise a child" became obsolete. In order to restore the action, we ALL must work in the trenches every day while searching for solutions, instead of making excuses. The assignment has been frequently misunderstood. We have to begin by creating the mindset, shifting the climate and culture to empower our youth to move forward, onward, and upward!

Whichever chapter you are going through in your life at the moment, remember to appreciate the people who are apart of the jOURney, Whether they provide positivity or negativity, inspiration or acts of manipulation, trust the process and your instincts to evaluate everything around you. Believe it or not, there is valuable knowledge to be gained in every situation. Intrinsic or extrinsic motivation both can move you forward, onward and upward.

CONCLUSION

Here we are, at the end of our journey, or more precisely, at the beginning of a new journey. I hope you have been convinced to incorporate The Playbook of Principles for Principals and its related competencies into your current or future leadership roles. This playbook contains the elements that can make individuals become good principals. As a result, the impact a good principal has on a school is more vital and broader than previously considered, making it difficult to imagine what would be a better return on investment in education than cultivating high-quality school leadership. Let's ensure your school is a better place for students, faculty, staff, and stakeholders to grow. Let's strive to improve our school and make it a better place: by becoming more competent and kinder, by becoming more understanding, by becoming more insightful, and by becoming more collaborative. The best way to encourage your students, faculty, staff, and stakeholders is to continually push them to become whomever they want to be in this world, no matter what it may be. You can keep this thought with you daily as a leader as you strive to move every student forward, onward, and upward in every school, community, and every day of your life.

SUPPORT SUPPORT SUPPORT

I have a conflicted relationship with the word "support." Supportive principals are often described with cheerful, reverent tones -- as in, "It is a dream to have a principal who is always supportive of me," and "Unsupportive principals are the worst."

I wanted to be known as a supportive principal. Firstly, it is essential to ask ourselves what exactly "support" means to us?" The answer is multilayered. Throughout my career as a teacher, I believed that support meant my principal would always defend me. There was a time when I thought my principal should go out of their way to reassure me that I was correct, even if I had made a mistake. To me, that was supportive. Unfortunately, it gets mixed up with other words, meaning something different – defend, corroborate, implicate, fortify, secure, or reassure. Principals and teachers expect support from each other, but they want unquestioned loyalty.

An alternative definition of the word would be helpful. The goal of support should be to question one another with respect, kindness, and an open mind. By doing so, we should keep an eye on growth, be available to change, and respect our colleagues' professionalism. There is an evolution, a process, and an end goal to support. The verb should be an action, a dynamic process symbiotic with the noun.

This example illustrates what we mean when we say we'd like support and what is the best way to offer and receive it.

Supportive principals do not have cliques or favorites among their students. Bullying is not something they do. Instead, their approach seeks multiple perspectives and offers a framework for assisting teachers. Teachers understand that their purposes, priorities, and patterns may change. Despite being patient, they don't fear challenging the status quo. It is well known to them that support is based on relationships. The combined energy can be funneled into the student support system with a supportive principal-teacher connection.

REMEMBER, YOU WERE A TEACHER.

Many principals were teachers before they became principals. Hence, the best thing a principal can do to support their teachers is to make administrative decisions that come from the teacher's hearts to inspire them. The administrator should have the best interests of the staff in mind when running a school with the heart of a teacher. Consequently, they ensure teachers develop as leaders by doing whatever it takes. Professional development activities are offered, and teachers are also allowed to lead.

Our colleagues up and down the halls teach us the most. By encouraging their staff to share knowledge and expertise, school administrators create an environment conducive to success and a group of colleagues willing to work together. To ensure a positive school culture, an administrator plays a key role. As well as modeling for teachers who might one day become administrators themselves, that administrator serves as an example for them. So let's fill school districts with principals who care because they remember their classroom days! What a difference that could make in our schools.

COACH YOUR TEACHERS.

One of the best things a principal can do is to be a strong instructional leader and coach their teachers. As the instructional leader of the campus, it is up to the principal to build a culture of learning and growing at the campus. Every teacher at every level of experience deserves a coach. All teachers should be given multiple opportunities to expand their knowledge, learn more Effective instructional strategies, and improve their teaching practices.

Part of running a school with the heart of a teacher means that the administrator has the staff's best interests in mind. Therefore, they do whatever it takes to ensure teachers grow as leaders. They offer professional-development activities and allow teachers to lead as well. We learn the most from our colleagues up and down our hallways. Administrators who encourage school staff to share expertise create an atmosphere conducive to success and a group of colleagues with buy-in in the workplace.

An administrator leading with the heart of a teacher is essential to ensure a positive school culture. But also, that administrator is modeling for teachers who may become administrators themselves someday. Let's fill school districts with principals who care because they remember their classroom days! What a difference that could make in our schools.

ABOUT THE AUTHOR

PRINCIPAL "COACH" RONNIE HARVEY, JR

ABOUT THE AUTHOR

Introducing Ronnie Wayne Harvey, Jr., also known as Principal Coach Harvey (PCH), an esteemed and esteemed educator, speaker, and author who works for the Calcasieu Parish School Board in Lake Charles, Louisiana. With 18 years of experience in education and various leadership roles, Principal Coach Harvey has demonstrated his ability to lead transformation and has been recognized with several prestigious awards. Principal Coach Harvey has an impressive educational background, having graduated from the prestigious University of Louisiana at Lafayette with a Bachelor of Arts in Speech Pathology & Audiology and a master's degree in education from Louisiana Christian University. His extensive experience in education has been primarily centered around his service as the principal of Calcasieu Parish Alternative Sites. In this role, he has played a vital role in supporting children facing various challenging circumstances.

Principal Coach Harvey deeply understands that each student has unique needs and motivations for alternative education. To better address their requirements, they conducted thorough research to identify universal necessities essential to helping these children overcome difficulties. His comprehensive approach has proven highly effective, as they have successfully assisted numerous children in overcoming various challenges and achieving academic successes. Realizing that each student had unique needs and reasons for alternative schooling, he researched and gathered that universal requirements include a firm grasp of adolescent brain development and trauma-informed care and a focus on skill building while building academic skills and school connections. As a result, PCH created an emphasis on skill building. Identifying the goals the youth, family, and school wanted to achieve and skills to build to assist with long-term behavioral change. PCH also recognized opportunities that exist in his community by re-engaging adolescents. This was monumental in ensuring that youth are reaccepted and reintegrated well into their home school when they return.

Furthermore, he offered continued support – recognizing that students who have been through an alternative program will need to continue to follow up and have a person "in their corner," perhaps throughout their academic/social life, as the principal of Washington Marion Magnet High School. Mr. Harvey aspires to shift the climate and culture of the school while empowering the surrounding community. In his first year of being named principal, Washington Marion's overall school performance score was 61.2. Understanding that a strategic and unorthodox approach was needed, Mr. Harvey immediately recruited, hired, and retained highly certified teachers and support personnel. An action plan was created, and it contained a strategy for improving school culture, with an understanding that he had to be clear about the values and traditions central to the school community. Harvey understood that effective leadership practices, including data-driven decisions, were vital in moving the school forward. In little over a year, Washington Marion grew 14.9 points, resulting in a school performance score of 76.1. Washington Marion has experienced a significant increase in enrollment, graduation rate, and all students departing college and career ready. Mr. Harvey aims to continuously move his school and community forward by educating all stakeholders about graduation pathways, increasing the availability of STEM and robotics programs on campus, and remaining transparent in all aspects of the school and its pulse. Mr. Harvey always aspired to shift the climate and culture of the school while empowering the surrounding community. He was also recently elected to the Lake Charles City Council to represent District A, the same district he was born, raised, worked in, and currently resides in with his wife, Shavela, and twins Paytleigh Dare and Ronnie III.

Made in the USA
Monee, IL
31 July 2023

40236786R00095